T0340010

The Medical Phraseology Guide for Superior Patient Safety

The Medical Phraseology Guide for Superior Patient Safety

How to Improve Communications Between Caregivers

Jérôme Cros

Routledge
Taylor & Francis Group
A PRODUCTIVITY PRESS BOOK

First published 2021
by Routledge
600 Broken Sound Parkway #300, Boca Raton FL, 33487

and by Routledge
2 Park Square, Milton Park, Abingdon, Oxon, OX14 4RN

Routledge is an imprint of the Taylor & Francis Group, an informa business

Library of Congress Cataloging-in-Publication Data

A catalog record for this title has been requested

ISBN: 9780367652487 (hbk)
ISBN: 9780367652463 (pbk)
ISBN: 9780367652609 (ebk)

Typeset in Garamond
by Deanta Global Publishing Services, Chennai, India

To Hélène, Philomène, Juliette and Augustine
Always seeking to offer you the right words at the right time.

Contents

Foreword

In March 1977 two Boeing 747 "Jumbo-Jets" collided on the runway in Tenerife in what remains the worst air disaster in history. As with most accidents, there were a large number of factors that delivered everyone involved to the brink of disaster: the pressure of unexpected external events, inclement weather, time delays, commercial pressure, a lack of fail-safe systems to provide an overview of the airfield movements, unfamiliarity, the physical environment, etc.

Despite all this, there was a final line of defense that the passengers could have faith in: the flight crew of the two jets, highly trained and competent individuals with thousands of hours of flying experience.

Yet the final line of defense failed.

Communication between Air Traffic Control and one of the airplanes, and subsequently amongst the crew of that airplane, resulted in confusion about a clearance to take off. The situational awareness of the crew wasn't shared amongst all members, and despite an attempt to seek clarity by two junior members of the team, the captain commenced the takeoff, enveloped in thick fog. Just as the captain lifted the nose of their graceful blue-and-white 747 into the grey sky, they collided with the second 747 that was taxiing on the runway. 583 died.

This accident brought a fundamental change to communication phraseology in aviation. As you read this, every flight today by every flight crew around the world will have used two phrases that have been standardized as a result of this disaster. The phrase "take off" is only ever used when a crew is actually cleared to take off; any other time communications refer to "departure". This subtle change could have saved 583 lives in 1977.

In March 2005 my late wife attended hospital for a routine procedure. She was anaesthetized and slipped into unconsciousness. She never woke up. A small range of factors conspired to take her to the brink of disaster: pressure, a lack of fail-safe processes, unexpected events, unfamiliarity, etc.

Despite all this, there was a final line of defense that Elaine, our children, and myself could have faith in: the clinicians, highly trained and competent individuals with years of experience.

Yet the final line of defense failed.

Communication between the medics became unclear and stilted, confusion about what was happening, what it meant and what needed to happen were never clarified. The situational awareness of the team wasn't shared amongst all members, despite attempts by two junior members of the team to clarify and intervene. It took Elaine 13 days to die.

The science of communication is relatively well understood in other safety-critical industries. We understand the importance of terminology, when to use certain words and when not to use certain words. We recognize that when pressure increases, and time is short, communication is the one thing that can bring a team back from the brink of disaster – and even better, can help keep us away from the brink in the first place.

This excellent work by Jerome is, to the best of my knowledge, the very first attempt to offer an insight into a topic that is essential for those who work in healthcare. Modern healthcare spends much time teaching you how to communicate with patients. But the most critical conversations that will keep your patients safe will be the ones you have with your colleagues.

Captain Martin Bromiley OBE, FRCSEd (ad hom)
Founder, Clinical Human Factors Group

Foreword

Life is often strange and offers us echoes full of coherence as time passes.

In the 1990s, I was responsible for the European Civil Aviation Authorities project reflecting the benefits of academic studies accumulated since the 1940s on human error, particularly those related to communication between cockpit crew members. At that time, statistics already showed that more than 50% of air accidents were related to inappropriate behavior, poor cooperation and non-standardized communication, which exposed crew members to kinds of possible interruptions and errors. To reduce this risk, Crew-Resources Management training to improve cooperation and communication has become an essential part of mandatory pilot training.

But make no mistake, the subject of communication is vast, very vast, and much more complex to teach than we imagine.

Communication is not only an exchange of words, of meaning, of a sender–receiver arrangement, it also carries the essence of all social and cooperative life in its tone, in its timing, in the listening and availability it demands from the other, in the words chosen, in the words which are not said voluntarily and the words which are implicit (what we no longer need to say but that the other guesses).

Nothing is really new in this field; the fundamental theories and achievements in communication are already several decades old. Shannon and Weaver's famous transceiver model dates back to 1949 and its optimization in Berlo's model – which adds the central role of context in the transceiver relationship – dates back to 1960.

But it remains true that any industry, any social activity, any team and any human relationship, including the intimacy of lovers and the bonds within a family, needs effort and a framed language tool to settle and last over time.

In this world of language complexity, nothing is innate, spontaneous, or effective from the start. Apprenticeship and training are necessary. We can walk and talk … but we are all largely unequal in the practice of this basic knowledge. This is the lesson of all the industries that have wanted to make progress in this area.

Aeronautics, which is so often cited, took 20 years to take notice of university research and impose it in training for all its professionals with validated pedagogical standards. The nuclear, chemical and oil industries, which use guided transport, have followed these contributions with a delay of more than ten years. In each area a work of adaptation and implementation was necessary.

It is now the turn of medicine, and this is good. There, as elsewhere, more than 50% of healthcare-associated adverse events (CAEs) are related to cooperation and poor communication. And it will come as no surprise to anyone reading this book that anesthesia is at the forefront of the production of ideas and educational concepts. This specialty has succeeded, for the past ten years, at transferring human factors concepts into the medical field.

This book is a delight, an unparalleled sum of experience that combines theoretical knowledge along with everyday examples, and that will make sense for all professionals.

This is not the first contribution to the subject; we are thinking, for example, of the Situation Background Assessment Recommendation (SBAR) grid which has already been recommended for standardizing medical language at the international level; but it is by far the most complete contribution, and the most accessible to all.

Thank you to Jérôme Cros for this valuable contribution, which comes at the right time for changing minds and putting the necessary rigor into improving collective work in medicine.

Shannon, C. & Weaver, W. (1949). *The mathematical theory of communication. Urbana*, USA: University of Illinois Press.
Berlo, D. (1960). *The process of communication*, New York, USA: Holt, Rinehart and Winston Inc.

René Amalberti, Prof, MD, PhD

Acknowledgments

This book summarizes the findings of many years of practice, thinking and various collaborations.

Thanks to Thomas Geeraerts and Bruno Bastiani for their support and precious advice.

Thanks to all anesthesiologists from the Mother-Child Hospital in Limoges: Anne Vincelot, Patrick Sengès, Claire Mancia, Catherine Chapellas, Baher Youssef, Charles Hodler, Daniel Berenguer and François Gauthier—an outstanding team that supports me and keeps inspiring me.

Thanks to all those who accompanied me during the years of simulation: Thomas Fauvet, Matthieu Charpentier, Guillaume Gilbert, Gaëlle Gaine, Antoine Bedu, Cyrille Catalan, Marie-Noëlle Voiron, Abdelilah Tahir, Vincent Guigonis, Gilles Pihan, Jérôme Gaillard, Christine Bourdeau, Laurent Fourcade, Quentin Ballouhey, Delphine Kabta, Franck Carbonne and once again Daniel Berenguer and François Gauthier.

Thanks to Nathalie Nathan-Denizot for trusting me.

Thanks to Gérard Béchonnet, who passed on his passion for pediatric and neonatal anesthesia.

Thanks to Pierre Beaulieu for sharing his energy, and to François Clapeau for making this book happen.

Thanks to the John Libbey Eurotext publishers for their unfailing support.

Authors

Jérôme Cros is an anesthesiologist and intensivist in Limoges, France. He is a trainer in health simulation and founder of the French group on human and organizational factors in healthcare.

Collaborator

François Clapeau is a journalist and health specialist. He has an MA in Health Management and Policies in the Political Sciences and has contributed to every step of the conception of this book. He has also published three novels – *Damage Control, Playoffs* and *Barré* (Editions Geste).

Translators

Thank you Eve Ysern and Alexia Herault Demuth for translating this from French to English.

Introduction

The lessons of aviation safety

In the 1970s, the civil aviation world was shaken by two major deadly plane crashes. Even greater was the trauma in the aviation field as there was no mechanical breakdown in any of the planes that could have accounted for such dramas. These accidents were due to human factors, although "human error" may be a better phrase to avoid disambiguation with the concept of human factors that is introduced later. The National Aeronautics and Space Administration (NASA) conducted a study on pilots that suggested using new simple rules regarding crisis management on a flight deck would be beneficial [1]. In 1993, David Gaba recommended transposing the principles of aviation crisis management to the operating room. The principles of Crisis Resource Management (CRM) follow those of aviation point by point [2, 3]. In the following years, more studies were conducted in order to assess the impact of human mistakes in the care field. In 1999, the Institute of Medicine published a report showing that in the United States, medical errors accounted for 50,000 to 100,000 deaths per year that could have been avoided [4]. This truly raised awareness. From then on, a lot of money was invested in order to fight human error. The World Health Organization (WHO) pointed out that the perioperative field was particularly vulnerable to this type of error. The Safety Surgery program was entrusted to Atul Gawande. The solution he offered in 2009 was once again inspired by the aviation sphere: the checklist [5].

Although no new medicine nor technique was proposed, the number of deaths was cut by half. The use of the checklist and CRM principles rely on a good level of communication among nursing staff. Several studies show that communication is often at the heart of undesirable events [6], especially in the operating room [7]. In the aviation field, communication is codified by a set of rules called "phraseology". These rules are elaborated and updated by the International Civil Aviation Organization (ICAO) [8]. In the health field, except for a few very specific tools [9], there are no such general rules. It would be a good thing to create a "medical phraseology" that would comprise clear, simple and precise rules presiding over the verbalized language used for care and that should be shared by all.

What Room for Phraseology in the Care Field?

At Aberdeen University in Scotland, psychologists noticed that theoretical knowledge, technical skills, or equipment problems are rarely the cause of accidents and incidents when attending a patient. Most of the time, the contributing factors are related to team organization, lack of situation awareness and the absence of verifications. The Aberdeen team then developed the idea of non-technical skills, which are very similar to those of crisis management developed by NASA and used by David Gaba.

Around the concept of non-technical skills, they built scores, particularly for anesthesiologists, surgeons, and nursing staff working in operating rooms.

For anesthesiologists, this score is called Anaesthetists' Non-Technical Skills (ANTS). This tool has now become a reference to assess the non-technical skills observed in a situation or simulation of patient care. It provides terminology that allows for the giving of feedback to student anesthesiologists.

Non-technical skills are classified into four major categories, each comprising three to six skills.

A global score out of 60 is obtained by giving each skill a grade ranging from 1 to 4.

Anaesthetists' Non-Technical Skills (ANTS) Score
TASK MANAGEMENT   • Planning and preparing   • Prioritising   • Providing and maintaining standards   • Identifying and utilising resources
TEAM WORKING   • Co-ordinating activities with team members   • Exchanging information   • Using authority and assertiveness   • Assessing capabilities   • Supporting others
SITUATION AWARENESS   • Gathering information   • Recognising and understanding   • Anticipating
DECISION MAKING   • Identifying options   • Balancing risks and selecting options   • Re-evaluating

Elements of communication are to be found in many of the skills mentioned above, especially in the teamwork category. The most obvious "verbal" skill would be "exchanging information". However, all the other teamwork-related skills, either partly or entirely, depend on a verbal vector. Coordinating activities with the team requires communicating, and it is through spoken words that we can relay authority and assertiveness, specifically through our tone of voice. "Supporting others" and "assessing capabilities" also happens to be linked to the interaction between different team members, whether this communication is verbal or non-verbal.

Most of these non-technical skills share a link with "communication". For instance, regarding the "identifying options" skills (in the "decision making" category), the practical guide indicates that good behavioral markers are related to the ability to generate various options and discuss them with other anesthesiologists if necessary. As for the "recognizing and understanding" skill (situation awareness category), one of the good behavioral markers is to inform other team members of the seriousness of the situation.

Most of these rules are therefore communication rules.

They point out "what must be said", but not necessarily "how it should be said". Phraseology answers the "how" question.

In this book, 26 simple, concrete, and practical rules related to daily care are suggested. They are derived from:

- The transposition of aeronautical phraseology rules
- Existing rules
- Literature analysis on the subject
- Our observations in clinical practice
- Our observations of the session in the simulation laboratory
- Many exchanges with colleagues who shared their experiences with us

These rules will require extensive studies for their efficiency to be proven or discarded.

But should we wait for the outcome of long and complex clinical studies before we implement a few rules based on common sense, which have already proved useful in other contexts? Can't we draw conclusions from clinical cases we've been through with patients or in our simulation labs to learn how to better communicate? Other high-risk lines of work have already answered these questions. *Evidence-based medicine* has not yet confirmed the efficiency of the majority of the 26 rules you're about to read. In this way, they can be modified and adapted. Nevertheless, their goal remains to bring about reflections regarding medical way discourse and related potential changes of practice.

Chapter 1

The Message

In this chapter, we will address verbal interactions occurring between only two nursing staff members.

We will disregard times when more than two people interact, such as in team meetings, for instance. But even though the suggested rules are described as codifying interactions between two people, most are also valid in a group context.

In order to describe the message, two different contexts may be identified:

- an interaction when the two nursing staff members are in the same room
- a phone conversation

The suggested rules apply to both situations, with only slight differences according to the context.

The closest situation to the rules of aviation phraseology is a phone conversation between two caregivers. We suggest extending the use of these rules to face-to-face interactions when the two people are in the same room.

Define a Goal or Set an Objective

Several kinds of messages may be transmitted verbally in a care context.

What Kinds of Messages?

- The message may correspond to a verbal instruction, whether it is an order or a medical treatment.
- The message, also called a transmission, is important during the transfer of responsibility regarding patient care. Several scenarios are relevant [7]: change of unit; change in the group of care professionals; change of building; team turnover.
- Requests for advice are also typical situations of verbal exchange.
- The interaction may also be regarding organization, such as conversations about operating programs or tasks.

This first typology is specific to the care field.

Different types of messages conveying a specific goal can be classified using a universal rule, which may also apply outside the care field. Is the message sent:

- For information purposes?
- Because a specific action is expected?
- In order to get an expected answer?

Before saying anything, we should ask ourselves the type of message we intend to pass on. Thinking before communicating is a common subconscious process that allows us to be fully aware of our message, and thus to adjust it if necessary. This way, we (the sender) are able to use specific rules which are suited to the type of message we intend to pass on, and we can make its purpose clear to the recipient.

In the ER (Emergency Room)

☒ The intern (to his or her senior referent doctor): *"I'm calling you about Mrs. Doper, at 18 weeks of pregnancy. She has pain in her calf muscle, which is a little edematous, without any clear sign of deep vein thrombosis. Since she is pregnant, I'm not sure, but I'm thinking of transferring her to the maternity Emergency Room".*

This is what the senior doctor may understand:

- the intern only wants to share the information, and he/she is taking care of the problem;

  Or

- he/she is expecting help from me and wants me to examine the patient;

  Or

- he/she is asking for my opinion and needs my advice about what to do.

Therefore, the doctor may answer inappropriately, which could lead to suboptimal management.

☑ *"I'm calling you about Mrs. Doper. She is pregnant at 18 weeks of amenorrhea. She has a pain in her calf muscle, which is a little edematous, without any clear sign of phlebitis. Since she is pregnant, I'm not sure, but I'm thinking of transferring her to the maternity Emergency Room".*

Option 1: *"In your opinion, should we ask for a Doppler of the lower limbs before we transfer her? Or do we keep her here?"*

Option 2: *"Can you please come over and check for yourself to make sure that you have the same clinical impression as I do before the transfer?"*

Option 3: *"I just wanted to let you know".*

These three examples of possible messages are clearly defined. Each allows the recipient to better understand the sender, and to react accordingly.

> Frame the message

A framed message reflects a synthetic and rigorous thought.

Be Precise, Concise and Exhaustive

As in the aviation field, concise and accurate speech is encouraged when using a medical discourse. Precision, brevity and comprehensiveness are the basic qualities of the message, as taught in flight manuals [8]. However, in everyday medical language, we can detect numerous inaccuracies, which are potential sources of error.

In the Operating Room

☒ The anesthesiologist (to the nurse anesthesiologist): *"Go ahead, you can give him fluids"*. This message may be understood in different ways:

  – must the nurse give 250 ml of normal saline to start with?

  Or

  – must he/she keep administering fluids, as long as the blood pressure does not rise, which can result in dispensing several liters of saline?

In this case, the flaw concerns the quantity of medication.

☑ The anesthesiologist (to the nurse anesthesiologist): *"Give 500 ml of normal saline"*.

This inaccuracy may concern aspects other than a quantity of medicinal product; for example, a symptomatology.

In the Operating Room
☒ The anesthesiologist (to the nurse anesthesiologist): *"If the blood pressure goes down, give ephedrine".* One nurse may consider low blood pressure to be a systolic blood pressure of 60 mmHg, while another nurse may consider it to be at 100 mmHg. This is why the symptom must be detailed in figures when possible.
☑ The anesthesiologist (to the nurse anesthesiologist): *"If the mean blood pressure drops below 60 mmHg, inject 6 mg of ephedrine".*

Everything that is quantifiable must be quantified

In general, everything that can be measured in figures must be done so, including time.

Conciseness

Conciseness is also an important aspect of medical language for several reasons.

First of all, the shorter the message, the lower the risk of interruption. Also, a message is more likely to be listened to carefully and to be retained if it is short.

Comprehensiveness

Finally, a message must be exhaustive insofar as it must include all the necessary information and any omission may be a source of error.

Avoid the Metaphor

Metonymy is a stylistic device that replaces one concept with another through an underlying logical link. For instance, "the pen is mightier than the sword" actually means that words are more influential than violence. There is a logical link between the pen and the act of writing – this act is replaced by the tool that performs it. There is a shift in meaning here which, in medicine, may lead to an error [10].

In a Hospital Department
In clinical practice, it's common to replace the patient's name with his/her room number:

⊠ The nurse to the porter: *"Please bring 205 down to radiology"*. There is a logical link between the patient and the room he/she is in. This actually means: *"Please bring the patient from room 205 to radiology"*.
But this solution is no more satisfying as it leaves room for error regarding the patient's identity. In fact, the patient may have changed room, there can be two patients in the same room, or the room number may be wrong. Upon detecting a metonymy in the medical language – describing concept A using related concept B – it is important to clearly name concept A. Here, then, it is important for defining the patient's identity.

☑ *"Please bring Sophie Pages down to radiology"*.
Related concept B may be added to the patient's name as a precision if necessary, but should never replace it.
☑ *"Please bring Sophie Pages down to radiology; she's in room 205"*.

When transferring a patient to the maternity ward, the anesthesiologist says to his colleague taking over:

  ⊠ *"The preeclamptic woman from yesterday shows higher blood pressure. Please check on her this morning; we might have to give her antihypertensive IV agents"*.

There may be confusion, here, if two preeclamptic patients have been admitted.

It's also common, in medical language, to refer to a patient using his/her pathology. This may also result in an error as several patients located in the same area might show the same pathology. Metonymy is so widespread and normal that it can be hard to identify.

In the Operating Room

☒ *"There is an elbow in the ER; we need to operate tonight"*. Here there is a double metonymy:

- the anatomic zone replaces the name of the injury – the doctor should have used "right distal humeral fracture" instead of "elbow".

- the injury replaces the actual name of the patient.

☑ *"In the ER, there's a child, Julie Monat, who has a right distal humeral fracture; we need to operate her tonight"*.

Calling a patient by their name

A fellow doctor told me that he once put a 15-year-old boy under general anesthesia by mistake for a minor right wrist fracture, while another child, also 15 years old, was still waiting in the ER with a fracture that required surgery. The doctor had sedated "the 15-year-old boy with a wrist fracture in the ER".

On top of the potential security benefit, calling a patient by his/her name allows us to better grasp him or her as a person. When calling the patient by their name, we take their life, family, job and history into account. Whereas when calling the patient by their pathology, we see them as no more than an organ and limit care to its mechanical dimension. Even in their absence, calling a patient by their name is a sign of respect that humanizes care.

Use a Specific Verb

The verb is at the heart of the sentence and describes an action being performed by (or on) a subject. It may also refer to the situation or be used to modify the subject.

When referring to an action, a verb can be more or less specific.

In everyday language, the verb "to do" is used very often. However, it carries a minimal amount of information and may have different meanings.

In the Operating Room

☒ *"Give zero point one milligram of epinephrine"* The nurse may either:
 	
  – prepare a syringe containing adrenaline (with 0.1 mg in 1 ml) and consider his/her job done;
  Or
  – inject 0.1 mg of adrenaline.
 	
We noticed that this mistake was made quite often in the simulation room. Either the medication is injected when it shouldn't have been, or it is only prepared when it should have been injected.

☑ *"Prepare an adrenaline syringe at zero one milligram per milliliter"*. *Or* *"Inject zero point one milligram of adrenaline"*. Here, the verbs "prepare" and "inject" carry information that is not found in the verb "do".

Anesthesia in the Operating Room
A patient must have an emergency cesarean section under general anesthesia. The anesthesiologist just injected the hypnotic agent and the muscle relaxant agent, and the patient can therefore be intubated.
Then he says: ⊠ *"Go ahead!"* to the intern so she can intubate. On hearing these words, the surgeon makes the incision, thinking the instruction was meant for him: *"Go ahead"* meaning *"You can proceed with the surgery"*. For safety reasons, we would rather wait until a patient is intubated before making the incision.
☑ *"It's okay, Sophie, you can intubate"*. In this example, the verb "to go" is not specific enough. The verbs "to intubate" or "to make an incision", on the other hand, are meaningful.

A verb must describe an action or a specific situation

In the aviation field, an air traffic controller wouldn't say: *"It's okay, go ahead"*, but *"Cleared for take-off"*. All specific actions are designated using an appropriate and meaningful verb.

Customize the Contact (Triangle of the "Who")

Personalizing contact is a strong and well-applied rule in aeronautics during radio transmissions.

An analogy can be made with phone communications in care environments. In aviation, all messages start with the name of the sender directly followed by the name of the recipient. This is a key element that ensures the right message is delivered to the right person. However, this habit is only partially shared in medicine.

In any medical message, it is fundamental to clearly identify at least three people:

- the patient, by their name (as seen above);
- the sender, who must introduce themself along with their position;
- the recipient, whose name and job must be verified by the sender.

Knowing the name and job of the person we are speaking to will allow us

- to ensure we follow-up on information in cases where there are multiple messages regarding the same patient;
- to adjust our level of language to the level of expertise of the person we are speaking to;
- to avoid passing on medical information to someone who does not need it;
- to make sure that the person responsible for the patient received the information.

Drawing the Triangle of the "Who"

These key elements – name and job – are proposed first in the second stage of the World Health Organization's operating room checklist.

In order to fully grasp this idea of identifying the protagonists and the patient, the triangle of the "who" may be used (Figure 1.1). During an exchange, a caregiver must always consider if this triangle is well placed.

A caregiver = a name + a function

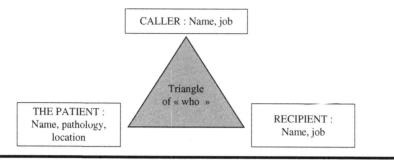

Figure 1.1   The triangle of the "who"

Locate, Temporize

In a message, elements of context may turn out to be fundamental: patient location and indications regarding the timescale for care.

Sometimes, when transferring a patient, it is necessary to mention the exact location where he or she is expected to be moved. As for timescale information, it may relate to the level of emergency, the history of the pathology or the care organization.

These elements of context may very well be implied and not spoken, resulting in delayed or unsuitable care.

Cardiac Arrest in the Maternity Ward

The midwife calls the on-call pediatrician:
☒ *"Come quickly; there's a newborn having a cardiac arrest!"*
Since most of these phone calls are received from the delivery room by the person "on-call", the pediatrician concludes, in spite of not having been given the information, that this is where the cardiac arrest is happening. Upon arrival at the delivery room, there is no cardiac arrest. He spends several minutes trying to find the newborn in the maternity ward. The midwife, in distress due to the emergency of the situation, forgot to mention the precise location of the newborn because she took it for granted that newborns are usually admitted to the maternity ward. This extremely delicate case highlights the importance of mentioning the patient's location.

> ☑ *"This is Veronica, a midwife on the maternity ward, sector 2. Come here at once, little Theo, born yesterday, is having a cardiac arrest, room 137".*

A patient = a location (or a transfer between two places)

In aviation, right after introducing him/herself, the pilot mentions where they are coming from and their destination; For example [11]: "SAU1234, 30 miles north of KOK VOR, FL80, KOK VOR at 21. Request clearance to cross airway V1 at KOK".

In order to reduce the time dedicated to the conversation and avoid confusion, we suggest setting up a protocol for every answered phone call. The answer must systematically start with the name, job and current location of the person receiving the call. For example:

> ☑ *"Hi, Rosa Lippmann, scrub nurse in operating room 28, speaking".*

As it is important to locate the care and the patient in space, it is also essential to locate them in time.

In a Hospital Facility
The nurse: "Hi, this is Hugo, the pediatric nurse. Lucas, a child admitted for chronic obstructive pulmonary disease, isn't feeling well; he's tachypneic and desaturating. Can you come over and check on him?"

The pediatrician: ⊠ "Yes, I'm going to check on him".
The nurse: "Okay, we're waiting for you".
The pediatrician's answer is ambiguous because it may mean either:
"I will stop what I'm doing, and I'll be right there".
Or
"Whenever I'm done with my consultation, I'll come and see him. As I have eight more patients to see, I'll be there in a couple of hours".

The pediatrician: ☑ *"Yes. I'll finish the consultation with the patient I'm seeing then I'll come up to the ward before I see the next patient. I'll be there in 15 minutes"*.
With this message, the nurse caller can organize their care and may express their disagreement if they consider that the degree of urgency is greater than the proposed intervention time frame.

Some recurring situations have already been identified as needing clear rules to determine the location and level of emergency of hospital care.

An emergency cesarean section may be coded red, orange or green. A code red indicates an extreme level of emergency and means that the cesarean section must be performed as soon as possible, within 15 minutes maximum, which some-times means performing the cesarean section in the delivery room. A code orange means that the emergency can't be postponed, although the anesthesia protocol may be adjusted, the patient may be transferred to an appropriate room and the time frame for action between the decision and the childbirth is extended to 30 minutes. Code green refers to a relative emergency and extends the time for intervention to 60 minutes.

In some life support services, the "emergency button" – a button located in the room – triggers a sound and light alarm system, which allows notifies all caregivers that there is an extreme emergency situation going on and indicates the rel-evant room.

Studies show [12] that the use of these rules improves care.

Formulate deadlines

Accompany the Figures of the Appropriate Unit

In medical language, we use a lot of quantitative information expressed in figures. These figures may describe:

- a symptom (blood pressure, diuresis, the size of a tumor, etc.);
- "machine-related" parameters (ventilation settings on a ventilator, section thickness on a CT-scan, dialysis adjustments, etc.);
- what a patient is treated with (dose of X-ray received in radiology or radiotherapy, medications, whatever the route of administration, etc.).

When it comes to verbalized prescriptions, confusion is frequent. A prescription may be given in vials, mg or ml. If a figure is used with no further precision, the person ordering the prescription and the person giving the medicine might not agree on the unit.

In the Pediatric Operating Room with an 8 kg Child

The anesthesiologist (to the anesthesiologist nurse or assistant):
☒ *"Give two of sufenta".*
In the anesthesiologist's mind, this means "2 µg of sufenta".
However, sufentanil is very often prepared at 5 µg per ml (standard dilution for an adult). Therefore, this verbal prescription is often given in ml. The anesthesiologist was actually injecting 2 ml of sufentanil at 5 µg per ml, which corresponds to 10 µg (5 times the recommended dose). This mistake had no major impact on the patient. But according to the age and weight of the patient, and depending on the medicine this confusion may carry much heavier consequences.

☑ *"Inject 2 micrograms of sufenta".*
Or
"Inject 2 milliliters of sufenta at 1 microgram per milliliter".

Another similar mistake, unfortunately quite prevalent, may have more serious consequences.

Tibia Fracture in the ER
A 10-year-old child arrives with a tibia fracture due to a skiing accident.

The physician tells the nurse: ☒ *"Give one of morphine".*
The physician means 1 mg of morphine. A vial contains 10 mg.
The nurse should have diluted the vial in 10 ml in order to dilute at 1 mg/ml and inject 1 ml. But in the nurse's mind, "one of morphine" meant 1 vial.
Therefore, the nurse injects the entire vial of morphine, which is 10 mg: ten times the correct dose ... the child becomes apneic and requires additional care.

☑ *"Inject 1 milligram of morphine".*
Or
"Dilute 10 milligrams of morphine into 10 milliliters and inject 1 milliliter".

A figure, a unit

Some figures don't have a proper unit, such as figures expressing a score or a relation; in biology, for instance, this includes the activated partial thromboplastin time (aPTT).

It's necessary to mention the score or relation of these figures:

- The aPTT is 1.2 times the control
- INR is 3.2
- His/her Glasgow is 13

A figure linked to a unit may seem like precise information, whereas actually it's only partial or incomplete. Some numbers thus need to be contextualized.

In an Intensive Care Unit, During the Morning Round
The physician as he/she is leaving: ☒ *"He has peed 400 milliliters"*. This sentence may seem clear enough because the figure mentioned has a unit. However, if this diuresis is collected over 12 hours for a patient weighing 80 kg, it is inferior to 0.5 ml/kg/h, which is abnormally low (oliguria). If this diuresis is collected over 3 hours for a patient weighing 50 kg, then it's superior to 2.5 ml/kg/h, which is normal. Regarding diuresis, what matters to the physician is the output.
☑ *"Over the last 12 hours, M. Schmidt's diuresis has been 0.8 ml/kg/h"*.

As with most rules of phraseology, as a group of people, we seek accuracy in communication in order to avoid accidents. This rule, therefore, does not apply only to the issuer.

If the message isn't precise enough, then it's the recipient's responsibility to make sure he/she understood the message and to ask for extra information if not (cf. Chapter 3).

Limit the Use of Acronyms

In medical language, acronyms are widespread. Written language has "contaminated" the way we use spoken language.

Acronyms have many advantages. In a written article about the central venous catheter, the use of the acronym CVC, defined in the introduction, is truly beneficial in terms of legibility. In a medical file, whether it's been written on a computer or handwritten, a "good" acronym may also facilitate reading and reduce the time spent on writing. For instance, PRC for packed red blood cells, FFP for fresh frozen plasma, etc.

When we talk, the use of an acronym is more difficult to justify: it's quite risky, as acronyms need to be learned, and their understanding demands acculturation.

The Receiver May Incorrectly Understand the Information

An acronym may have several different meanings. For instance, the acronym ARF may mean "acute renal failure" or "acute respiratory failure".

Misunderstanding may also happen with very similar acronyms: VT for ventricular tachycardia and DVT for deep vein thrombosis.

This issue exists in air safety, as well. The book *Fatal Words* gives an example of an error of communication due to the use of an acronym [13].

Upon landing, the controller says: *"We have the REIL [Runway End Identifier Lights] lights up"*.

The pilot, who isn't familiar with the acronym, understands that real lights are up *"We have the 'real' lights up"*. This incident of communication had no consequences, but it was reported in a magazine meant for pilots in order to keep such a situation from happening again and causing an accident.

The Receiver May Miss a Piece of Information

An acronym may make sense to the sender, but not to the recipient. This is especially true for acronyms whose use is limited to a certain group of people: locally and according to their specialty or level of experience.

"This patient has a COLD", might refer to a common cold or a Chronic Obstructive Lung Disease.

When pronouncing "CVP line", we may suppose that 90% of the caregivers understand that it means "central venous pressure line". But when we say, "central venous catheter", 100% of them understand it. A young student may ignore the acronym CVC, whereas it's obvious to the more experienced other caregivers. And this young student might not dare ask what it actually means.

Language is in Constant Motion

New medical concepts appear in the literature on a regular basis, and they often come with their own acronyms. Their meaning mustn't be taken for granted by any of us. During staff meetings, their use can lead to misunderstandings, and therefore errors.

Sharing one's knowledge implies sharing a common way to express it.

The Transmitter–Receiver Exchange Loses Meaning

The term ectopic pregnancy is much more explicit and visual than its acronym EP. The simple act of speaking all the words of an acronym opens our minds; it humanizes the care, the caregiver and the patient.

It's not necessary to totally ban acronyms from our spoken medical language. Some of them are so prevalent that they have replaced the actual names: MRI for Magnetic Resonance Imaging. This doesn't appear to cause any major problem; however, when we're speaking, it's best to limit the use of acronyms and be fully aware of those we're using.

We should also keep in mind that using acronyms in front of a patient may lead them to think we're trying to hide something from them. If we're speaking with colleagues in front of a patient, we must adjust our language in order to help them understand what's going on. The use of acronyms will disrupt this understanding.

Use Structured Methods

When a message is complex or critical, it's recommended that we use a structured communication method, for it allows us to be more comprehensive and efficient.

Several structured methods may be used. The most famous is the *Situation Background Assessment Recommendation* (SBAR) method.

First used by the US Navy, "SBAR" is a structured communication technique which caregivers started using a few years ago [14]. SBAR is an easy-to-remember mechanism useful for framing any conversation, and unfolding through four steps.

First Step: Situation

The situation is about defining "who", "what", "where".

"Who" is the patient, "who" is the person calling, "who" is the person called. "Where" is the patient, and possibly "where" must they go. These two rules aren't specific to the SBAR, but the SBAR starts with them.

"What" is the call sign. It mustn't be a diagnosis and can't be limited to "what's the problem?" In fact, two answers could be given regarding the same patient: "chest pain" or "suspected myocardial infarction". The correct wording is "chest pain", going directly to a conclusion would prevent the caller from following the caller's reasoning.

The person calling must state his/her name and job, make sure they are talking to the right person and mention the patient's name (see Figure 1.1).

Then he/she must mention the patient's location and the call sign, the first symptom or the event that drew their attention.

Second Step: Background

The patient's relevant history should be explained, depending on the case.

Upon calling an orthopedist about an ankle fracture, mentioning a previous fracture in the same place is relevant. However, mentioning this past ankle fracture to a cardiologist regarding suspicion of myocardial infarction would be irrelevant.

The patient's usual treatments are considered part of his/her medical background.

The context also includes the recent history of the patient and their illness, such as the events that occurred during the past few days. We may describe a car accident or mention what has happened since he/she was admitted.

Third Step: Assessment

This third step is the central aspect that will shape the conclusion.

The clinical exam is part of the assessment and may include: skin signs, respiratory signs, monitoring, blood pressure ....

The patient's complaints and his/her perception of pain must be taken into account. Any piece of information from additional medical examinations – biology, imaging – may be mentioned as well. We may also describe the previous treatments that have been given. Lastly, it's necessary to mention the evolution of the patient's condition. This stage of assessment ends with the conclusion.

The Conclusion Mustn't Come Earlier in the Course of Communication

Starting a conversation with a conclusion is a prevalent mistake. Without any further explanation, it might be dismissed or misunderstood by the recipient of the message and result in a waste of time. Here there is a fundamental difference between the initial "what". This initial "what" mustn't be questionable, for it's a fact. On the contrary, the conclusion is the outcome of medical reasoning. It may be a diagnosis, one or several diagnostic assumption(s) or just the reflection of the caregiver's main concerns.

Last Step: Recommendation

The caller explains what he/she needs and makes a request: an action to be undertaken, phone instruction, opinion... If we want the interlocutor to come over, we must be precise about the deadlines ("I need you in 5 minutes").

The health authority in France promotes this concept and calls it SBAR. The advantage of this acronym is that it is easy to remember; it will be necessary on the other hand not to limit the second step to the patient's past medical history only, but to add some notions of the history of the disease and recent anamnesis. Throughout our sessions at the simulation lab, we carried out simulations involving hundreds of participants who weren't familiar with the SBAR tool. We asked them what information a phone call regarding healthcare should contain.

Disregarding a few exceptions, most of the six-to-ten-people groups who were part of the experiment would mention all the elements included in the SBAR. The only element that was incomplete now and then was the Recommendation, usually because a time-limit for the suggested action was missing.

However, a lot of the time, elements would be mentioned in a random and disorganized order.

SBAR doesn't bring in any new elements compared to those already used by caregivers. But SBAR does add structure to the communication. This method is also useful because it's action-oriented. However, the method requires preparation before communicating. When picking up the phone, the caller must ensure that he/she has all the necessary elements at hand. Besides, this tool has proved to be helpful for cutting down mortality rates [15].

Other structured communication methods exist, such as "SOAP" (*Subjective, Objective, Assessment, Plan*), which allow us to follow a patient with consistent updates, or the "ANTICipate" (*Administrative data, New information clinical update, Task, Illness, Contingency planning code status*), which structures the patient's transfer process [16].

The use of care protocols has shown its effectiveness in the management of many pathologies. Structural tools such as SBAR represent real communication protocols.

Situation
Background
Assessment
Recommendation

Avoid the Implied

Cultural barriers and fear of being ridiculed tend to prevent us from saying out loud what seems obvious. Nevertheless, an implied message may result in an error: two people talking to each other aren't always on the same page.

We should ban every implicit element from our speech and express our ideas in a clear and straightforward manner. This is the safest way to avoid any suggestion coming from a deduction.

DIVERGENCE OF OPINION

A steward is appointed as the chief of staff for the first time on a long-haul flight. During the flight, as the aircraft is flying at cruising altitude, the pilot calls him into the cockpit. Pointing his finger straight ahead, the pilot tells him: "Look!" The steward notices thick clouds in the sky. As he goes back to the cabin, he makes an announcement telling the passengers to remain seated and keep their seatbelts fastened because the aircraft is about to cross an area of turbulence.

The pilot calls the steward back. He shows him more specifically a crack in the cockpit's front window; he actually wanted the steward to get ready for a possible depressurization.

The pilot should have said: "Look, there's a crack in the window; we have a depressurization risk situation".

Verbalize even what seems obvious

Septic Shock in the ER
A patient is admitted for peritonitis, complicated by septic shock: the situation is life-threatening in the short term.
There are two pressing emergencies: to inject antibiotics and to move the patient to the operation room. The emergency physician standing by the patient's bed makes a phone call to the anesthesiologist in the operating room.

The emergency physician: *"It's septic shock originating from the digestive system; I think he needs to be given Ceftriaxone, Metronidazole, Gentamicin"*.
The anesthesiologist: *"Okay, Ceftriaxone, Metronidazole, Gentamicin sounds good"*.
The emergency physician: ☒ *"Can I send him to you at the operating room right now?"*

The anesthesiologist: ⊠ *"The room is available; you can send him in".* After surgery, the nurse receiving the patient calls the anesthesiologist to find out what time the antibiotics were injected. He answers that the injection was done in the ER. When calling the ER, the nurse is told that the injection was done in the operating room. The nurse then realizes that there was no antibiotics injection at all. This is a serious mistake that may reduce the patient's chance of survival.

The emergency physician did think of the antibiotics but didn't want to waste any more time on injections. Thus he/she sent the patient to the operating room at once in order not to delay the surgery. When the anesthesiologist agreed on the choice of antibiotics, he thought he was approving their actual injection. These two caregivers were not sharing the same mental frame regarding the time and place of the injection.

The anesthesiologist: *"The room is available; you can send him in".*
The emergency physician: ☑ *"Are you going to inject the antibiotics?"*
The anesthesiologist: ☑ *"Give him the Ceftriaxone; I'll take care of the Metronidazole and the Gentamicin".*

Other similar circumstances can be found in the healthcare field.

What seems obvious to you is not necessarily obvious to your colleague.

Write Things Down

Hospital care involves many professionals working on different teams, sometimes even in different places. A communication chain must be set up to ensure continuity in the care process as information is transferred. A missing link in the communication chain is a source of possible error. In order to avoid such a situation, several solutions are suggested [7]: communication standardization, reinforced teamwork and simulation training.

Regardless of the quality of the orally transmitted message, "word of mouth" may change or cause an error in the message contents. Pieces of information may be lost or become inaccurate.

MYOCARDIAL SIDERATION

A 38-year-old patient who had a postpartum hemorrhage during her first delivery is admitted during her second pregnancy because she has minimal bleeding, with a covering placenta. The caregivers decide to perform a cesarean section under spinal anesthesia early in the morning.

During this cesarean section, after delivery of the baby, a severe hemorrhage develops, followed by a cardiac arrest probably due to an amniotic fluid embolism. Cardiopulmonary resuscitation is immediately initiated; in the absence of a return of spontaneous circulation 55 minutes after the beginning of the cardiac arrest, the patient is connected to a heart-lung bypass machine by the mobile circulatory support unit.

Acute critical care is pursued for hours for hemorrhage control in conjunction with circulatory support management. Late in the afternoon, the patient is transferred by ambulance to the cardiac surgical intensive care unit. In the evening, intra-abdominal bleeding is observed that requires expedient surgery to control the hemorrhage. Over the following days, the patient is progressively weaned from circulatory support.

The patient is transferred back to the intensive care unit in the hospital where the delivery took place. In the meantime, the attending team in the intensive care unit has changed. On the night of the transfer, this team feels the patient is fit enough for a step-down from the intensive care to the intermediate care unit.

During the morning rounds, the attending physician notices the fact that her medical record does not mention the term "cardiac arrest". Instead, it mentions the term "myocardial stunning". The attending intensive care team is not aware that the patient had suffered a prolonged cardiac arrest.

Myocardial stunning may indicate that the patient was given mechanical circulatory support, but it refers to a completely different diagnosis. Fortunately, this transmission mistake had no consequence on the patient, who went back home 15 days after the cesarean section without any neurologic sequelae. However, I spent a lot of time thinking over the causes of this mistake which may seem huge as it concerns the principal diagnosis.

The patient's medical record was well documented regarding the treatment in the cesarean section room (vital signs monitoring, the medicines used at different times), but showed no synthetic medical observation of the incident, probably because the physicians were busy with other tasks. However, the doctors had performed transesophageal echocardiography on the patient right before she was transferred, while the circulatory support mobile unit was already on its way. A written report of this exam had been made, and mentioned "myocardial stunning", which was accurate at that time: the cardiac activity had just slightly picked up (5 hours after the beginning of the cardiac arrest).

Between 40 and 50 people were involved in the patient's care: several caregivers for the cardiac massage, different anesthesiologists, an obstetrical-gynecological surgery team, a cardiac surgery team, midwives, anesthesiologist nurses responsible for the blood transfusion, etc.

The initial diagnosis was lost in the oral transmission which passed through about ten intermediaries. The written conclusion of the cardiac ultrasound then replaced the initial diagnosis.

Since then, every time a critical patient is transferred from the delivery room to the life support unit, a succinct written summary is required. Some teams have actually chosen to use written reports for all transmissions. However, we should weigh the pros and cons of this method because it does add workload. Each team should be able to make its own choice regarding the best way to ensure that transmissions are properly performed. Let's just keep in mind that there are limitations to oral transmissions – whatever their quality, whereas writing has proven to be more resistant to distortion and loss of information.

> The patient medical record is an element of communication

Chapter 2

The Attitude

Communication can be split into two categories: verbal and non-verbal. We just studied how to verbally transmit a message.

Non-verbal communication is perfectly integrated into the way we express ourselves; it's more difficult to control than verbal communication, and we tend to use it in a subconscious and automatic way [18].

Non-verbal communication is made of two parts: paraverbal communication and paralinguistic communication [19]. The first refers to the way the words are "dressed up": how we pronounce them, how fast we speak, etc. and covers everything "surrounding" the word. As for the second, it's more distant from the word in itself and refers to our body language: attitude, movements, facial expressions and looks.

Verbal	Non-verbal	
Words and sentences	Paraverbal	Paralinguistic
	Tone of voice, intonation, pace of speech	Movements, facial expressions, looks

In this section, we will cover non-verbal communication and the importance of the environment.

Use the Right Tone of Voice

Our tone of voice is meaningful: it conveys emotions. Beyond the words we use, our tone communicates our intention.

In the medical field, this notion takes us away from the patterns that are prevalent in aviation. In fact, the pilots' phraseology guide recommends using an unchanging tone of voice. Even the number of words spoken per minute is mentioned [8]. Their speech may then be very monotonous.

Within short and specific time frames, this can be very efficient. On the contrary, in healthcare, tone of voice could also be meaningful, convey information and allow us to separate what's important from what's not. "Errors in the tone of voice" may be observed. An inappropriate tone of voice may put up barriers and turn out to be detrimental to the communication.

A team member raising his/her voice in a threatening way means: "don't talk to me; don't contradict me". We might hesitate to speak up in front of a person using such a cold and strict tone of voice.

Moreover, an excessively aggressive tone of voice doesn't leave any room for shades of difference. It should be avoided. Aggression never helps a patient; it stuns the audience and paves the way for conflict.

On the contrary, a calm and clear tone of voice creates an atmosphere suited for efficient exchange. Without emphasizing polite small talk, one's tone of voice should always remain courteous and professional.

This way, the slightest difference may efficiently draw attention. In a calm atmosphere, raising our voice at a specific time may highlight the importance of what's being said.

One single sentence can affect the audience in different ways.

For example, a physician is talking to a student: *"Go ahead, find the vein and insert the cannula"*.

If the physician's tone of voice is benevolent, it will help the student's focus. He/she is implicitly told that there is no rush, which makes them feel safe. The same sentence, pronounced curtly, may convey a very different message: *"Hurry up, or I'll take over"*.

It seems difficult to establish a precise rule in this field: a lexical field can always give rise to interpretations, and it's impossible to measure a tone as we evaluate a quantity or a duration.

It is, however, fundamental to be aware that two messages that contain the same words may have different meanings according to the chosen tone of voice, which is also part of the message.

Clamp Removal in the Operating Room
The vascular surgeon just performed an aortic bypass. The stitching has been completed, and he/she's about to remove the aortic clamp. The surgeon has spent the last 15 minutes giving several instructions (instruments requests, light adjustments, etc.).

☒ In the same tone of voice, he says: *"I'm removing the aortic clamp"*.
The anesthesiologist, who hasn't been paying attention to previous instructions, misses this crucial piece of information. As a consequence, she/he is surprised to notice a blood pressure drop and the required actions are delayed.

☑ If the surgeon had pronounced the same sentence in a different tone than he used to give the previous instructions – preferably a pressing and authoritative tone of voice following a brief moment of silence – the anesthesiologist would have paid more attention to the message.

An appropriate tone of voice allows us to reduce stress and enhance a culture of safety, but may also be used as a tool to draw attention.

Diversifying and qualifying the tone of voice

Attract Attention when It's Important

The following medical case is the story of Elaine Bromiley's death. Her husband, Martin Bromiley, an airline pilot, describes the events and analyzes the causes of this tragic series of events through his expertise in aviation [20].

IMPOSSIBLE INTUBATION, IMPOSSIBLE TO VENTILATE

Elaine Bromiley is scheduled for sinus and nose surgery in March 2005. The pre-operative assessment revealed nothing unusual; the case was supposed to be a routine intervention; the anesthesiologist induced a standard general anesthesia induction sequence, and Elaine stops breathing. This is normal and expected after the induction of general anesthesia. The anesthesiologist attempted several times to secure the airway with a laryngeal mask to start mechanical ventilation. These attempts failed, and Elaine becomes hypoxic. Another attempt at mask ventilation failed as well, as does an attempt to control the airway with intubation. The nurses, the surgeon and a second anesthesiologist join him to help. The intubation attempts fail, and Elaine remains hypoxic. This is called a cannot intubate/cannot ventilate situation. It is a rare and critical situation that requires an emergency tracheotomy. However, the situation is not identified as such, and the tracheotomy is not performed. After several unsuccessful alternative technical attempts to control her airways, the operation is eventually canceled, and Elaine Bromiley is transferred to the recovery room. Thirty-five minutes elapsed between the beginning of the anesthesia and the transfer to the post-anesthesia care unit. The oxygen concentration in the patient's blood remained too low for too long, causing irreversible major hypoxic brain damage. Elaine never woke up and died 13 days after the event.

Relatively early in the intervention (before the 10th minute), a nurse announced: *"The tracheotomy set is available".* But she felt like she was being ignored. Later, two extra nurses confessed they were aware that a tracheotomy was necessary. We learn from an independent review that they didn't know how to bring up the topic, and several physicians claim they did not receive this piece of information.

A video recounting the events is available on the clinical human factors group's website.

During our simulation sessions, we played this video to hundreds of students, and systematically asked them the following questions: *"In your opinion, what's the level of accountability of the nurse who brought the tracheotomy set? Especially in regard to the physicians?"*

This question followed their answer: *"How could she have drawn the physicians' attention?"*

Regarding the first question, opinions tend to differ. Some professionals consider that the nurse spoke out and notified the physician that a tracheotomy was required; only the physician is responsible. Other caregivers have mixed feelings and simply think that the nurse should have insisted on the possibility of a tracheotomy. After discussions, a consensus prevails in favor of the second analysis. All groups emphasize how hard it is for a nurse to be heard by a physician in such a situation. The conclusion is, however, unanimous: regardless of his/her hierarchical position, each caregiver bears a moral responsibility towards the patient upon detecting an element unnoticed by his/her colleagues.

From then on, how do we draw attention to the issue? Several approaches arose from this discussion, with the idea of changing strategy if it proves inefficient.

- change tone of voice
- use relevant physical contact
- insist until we are certain we have been heard, ask for closing the loop
- wait for the right moment (according to the level of emergency)

In the aviation field, there is a list of keywords that are meant to draw attention to an issue and indicate an emergency situation at the outset, such as the famous *Mayday* and the less prevalent "pan pan". Used at the beginning of a communication, they refer respectively to a distress call and an emergency call. For the moment, there is no equivalent in medicine.

> Provide tools to draw attention

Observe and Optimize Body Language

The body speaks through gestures, looks, facial expressions and touch. Without saying a word, we can show our availability or need for attention.

MANAGEMENT OF PEDIATRIC
TRAUMATIC BRAIN INJURY

The simulation team follows the intervention of an experienced trainee, who is familiar with this exercise. From the outside, the observers think that she's very articulate: she efficiently transmits tasks to the nurse and explains her therapeutic goals in a simple and methodological way.

But during the debrief, there is a surprise: the nurse feels like the intern didn't communicate well. The observers in attendance are surprised and ask her to be more specific. She answers: *"I didn't feel heard. The intern was in her bubble, and I had the feeling she didn't hear what I was saying"*.

This is the type of issue that generates tension and an increased workload; it's logical that the intern wouldn't waste time on small talk.

The nurse is asked what sort of answer she would have appreciated. *"I would have liked her to look at me at that moment. It would have been enough for me to feel heard"*.

It's all about paralinguistic here. Everyone must grow aware of the fact that gestures and body attitude are key elements of communication. A specific emotional state may either entice us to communicate or, on the contrary, encourage us to keep quiet. This part of communication is very important: audio recordings of an intervention in the operating unit could never faithfully reflect all of the events that occur during an operation.

Regarding Elaine Bromiley's case, one of the nurses said that during the episode she had taken it upon herself to call the life support unit to book a bed. During the trial, she added that the physician then looked at her as if he were saying *"You're overreacting"* – which led the nurse to again call life support and cancel the reservation.

Gestures and eye contact are a part of communication

The physician didn't speak, but communicated through eye contact and thus pushed the nurse into making a critical decision.

Two lessons may be learned from this example. First, we can read into someone's look without them speaking. Second, we don't know what the physician really meant. Another nurse might have understood his look in a different way; hence, the importance of sending clear messages, even when using non-verbal communication.

Communication through gestures may nevertheless be relevant, particularly in a noisy or hectic environment: nodding to say yes, or place a finger on one's lips to ask for silence. Just as in scuba diving, it's possible to communicate efficiently without saying a word, insofar as we make sure that our gestures will be correctly interpreted.

Limit the Background Noise

In acute medicine, caregivers often work in noisy environments, such as emergency rooms, intensive care units, or operating rooms. A research study conducted in 2017 showed that clinical reasoning abilities are affected by noise. Once again, aviation has much to offer in terms of education. Lessons were especially learned from the accident in Tenerife [21].

A COLLISION BETWEEN TWO PLANES

On March 27, 1977, two Boeing 747s, one from KLM and the other from Pan American World Airways, collide at take-off from Tenerife airport in the Canary Islands. This is the deadliest accident in the history of the airline industry, with 583 people dead and 61 injured.

On this day, a bomb threat in Las Palmas airport diverts an unusually large number of aircraft toward Tenerife airport. There are significant delays and the two 747s are the last planes taking off that day. The crews are tense.

Shortly after 5 pm, the KLM plane is holding its position at the end of the runway waiting to take-off. The Pan Am plane is taxiing on the runway toward the take-off point. Both planes are facing each other, but can't see each other because of dense fog.

The Pan Am plane is supposed to turn left to reach a sidetrack and thus vacate the runway.

At 5.05 pm and 53 seconds, the air traffic controller passes the new route clearance to the KLM pilot. These are data related to the aircraft's flight path (after take-off). This is common practice. But it's not clearance for take-off. However, the pilot is thinking about tasks to be performed after the take-off and mistakenly believes that he's just been authorized to take-off.

At 5.06 pm and 9 seconds, the KLM pilot tells the air traffic controller: *"We are now at take-off"*. He pushes the power levers to accelerate, thinking the Pan Am plane has already left the runway. This pilot has a German cultural background and should have said, in proper English, *"We are now taking off"*.

The air traffic controller, who has a Hispanic cultural background, understands *"We are now ready to take-off"*, and doesn't stop the KLM aircraft.

At 5.06 pm and 18 seconds, the air traffic controller, thinking he's talking to a stationary aircraft, says *"Standby for take-off. I will call you"*. This sentence should have warned the KLM pilot, but it's interrupted by another radio transmission, unrelated. The two planes collide at 5.06 pm and 50 seconds.

The ICAO (International Civil Aviation Organization) radio-telephony users' manual suggests a list of rules to prevent this type of accident. If deemed necessary by the air traffic controller, he may call for silence, in general, or to someone in particular.

The same issue is to be found in healthcare.

IN THE ER, RESUSCITATION AREA

On this day, I'm an intern training at the French SAMU (French ambulance and emergency service). We're dealing with a motorbike accident. Our patient is in a state of acute hemorrhagic shock and we're driving him to the ER.

During transportation, the vascular filling isn't enough to maintain adequate blood pressure. We start adrenaline/epinephrine as a continuous infusion and brief the medical regulator on the pressing emergency of this case.

Three teams deal with the arrival of the patient in the crash room: life support, emergency and SAMU. The workload is significant from the outset. Transmissions are made between the 15 different professionals caring for the patient. Simultaneous interchanges of information between the members of different teams create an intense background noise.

A few minutes after the patient was admitted to the crash room, his blood pressure suddenly drops. While checking the adrenaline infusion, I realize that it was stopped by mistake as the syringe pump was given back to the SAMU. This is a major mistake that could have serious consequences on the patient's life.

Although the information about the adrenaline was transmitted, the people present in the room didn't perceive nor understand its importance. This mistake could have been easily prevented if communication had been standardized, and the background noise kept at a reasonable level. This way, transmissions could have been made without so many interferences. This also applies to "non-speaking" team members. In fact, this discipline compels everyone to listen to the same transmission, which must be clear, brief and precise.

Background noise may, therefore, come from care-related communications, not only unrelated communications – whether private or extraprofessional.

A recent research study showed that noise can affect care-givers capacities. The authors assessed the clinical reasoning performances of two groups of anesthesiologist interns. They had them take the *Script Concordance Test* (SCT). One group was exposed to a calm atmosphere, whereas the other was working in a noisy environment. Conclusion: the group exposed to noise underperformed. The younger the interns, the more significant the underperformance [22].

Background noise may come from a professional conversation or a non-professional one. It's not always related to words:

it can come from people tidying or handling instruments. Background noise can be harmful because of two major risks:

- someone could miss an important piece of information
- it could distract other caregivers

Therefore, it's fundamental to be fully aware of one's environment, and identify situations when background noise may cause interference.

Know how to be silent at the right time

Chapter 3

The Exchange

In aviation, however standardized the rules regarding phone calls may be in order to minimize the risks, communication failures still exist. No matter how far the rules go, there will always be mistakes.

They are categorized into three main types of communication failure [21].

Transmission of false information	In medicine, transmitting a piece of false information may result in confusion regarding a patient's identity, a medication, or dosage error ... It's an easy-to-identify mistake.
Loss of situation awareness	Loss of situation awareness may occur when an individual doesn't understand the vocabulary used by the person talking to him/her, for instance, because of the language barrier or a different specialty.
The absence of a shared mental representation of the situation	More complex is the absence of a shared mental representation of a situation. This time, it's related to a group of individuals. All care participants don't have the same understanding of the situation.

Before the Tenerife accident, upon taking off, when the KLM pilot says, *"We are now at take-off"*, his awareness of the situation could be summarized as "we're currently taking off; the runway is now clear". As for the air traffic controller's awareness of the situation, it comes down to *"they're ready to take-off, but waiting for the Pan Am aircraft to clear the runway"*.

Whatever the message or attitude, the exchange must make it possible to correct false information, obtain clarification and share the same awareness of the situation and the importance of care.

Close the Communication Loop

When a message is sent, it must be ensured that it has been received. The chain between the moment a message is issued and the moment it's understood may sometimes be complex, and mistakes may be made at any time.

An efficient way to let the person one's talking to know that the message has been received is to repeat it, partly or totally. In English, it's called *read-back*.

In the aviation field, its use depends on the importance of the information provided. For instance, direction, landing and take-off clearances will systematically read-back [8].

This method may allow for fixing a communication mistake: read-back can bring our attention to where our message is being misunderstood.

Read-back represents the safest way to close a "communication loop". In the aviation field, when receiving messages not considered essential, it's fine not to use read-back but instead answer:

- *Affirmative* for "yes"
- *Negative* for "no"
- *Roger* for "I acknowledge reception"
- *Wilco* for "I will comply" [8]

Some sentences such as *"go ahead"* are banned because of their ambiguity.

If the recipient fails to close the communication loop or when there is room for doubt, then it's the sender's responsibility to request closure.

In the aviation sector, specific words are used to request the closure of a communication loop, according to meaning and context:

- Acknowledge: *"Let me know that you have received and understood the message"* [8]
- Confirm: *"I'm asking for confirmation"* (regarding a clearance, instruction, action, information) [8]
- How do you read? : *"How clear is my transmission?"* [8]
- Read-back: *"Repeat, partly or totally, the message I just issued"* [8]
- Say again: *"Repeat, partly or totally, the message you just issued"* [8]

In the healthcare field, we intuitively use several methods to close communication loops, but erratically and in a non-standardized way: we may say *"Okay"*, nod or sometimes read-back. Yet confirming reception of a message is essential. It would, therefore, be worthwhile examining the best ways to do so according to the different contexts.

Climb the Ladder of Precision

Climbing the ladder of precision implies discussing and exchanging information until it is certain that everyone has the same understanding of the situation. It's about clarifying what is unclear and sometimes stating the obvious.

In a medical situation, it is necessary to ensure that the different protagonists in the conversation, telephone or direct, share the same vision of the situation.

Even if the outgoing message is correct, a caregiver may still need some clarification.

This attitude mustn't be perceived as a way to call the sender of the message into question, nor as a personal attack. On the contrary, it should be valued. In the course of these question-and-answer exchanges, participants should rid themselves of any hint of doubt. It's also about leaving room for discussion.

The image of the ladder is no random choice. Through a dialogue, two caregivers are allowed to climb, step by step, toward a high-level of shared knowledge.

Identify the blur

In the Resuscitation Room:
A patient suffering from head trauma is admitted to the crash room in a critical condition: he is in a coma. For this patient, the medical goals are multiple: the intensive care anesthesiologist must intubate him, sedate him, maintain normal blood pressure and perhaps use medication to reduce the intracranial pressure.
The physician also faces an organizational challenge. He must obtain a CT-scan report and prepare medical care in the operating room by making sure that a room is available, and a team is on hand to treat, for instance, a subdural hematoma.
Just before intubation, the radiologist gives the green light to proceed with the CT-scan exam. The intensive care anesthesiologist needs an extra 10 minutes to prepare the patient.

The intensive care anesthesiologist phones the neurosurgeon.
The intensive care anesthesiologist: ☒ *"I have a patient with critical head trauma in the crash room, I'm waiting for a CT-scan".*
The surgeon: ☒*"Okay, call me back when you have the images from the CT-scan".*
The surgeon has no precise idea of the patient's condition. Nevertheless, it would be relevant to start organizing potentially complex medical care. Together, both physicians should go further.

The intensive care anesthesiologist: ☑ *"Good morning, it's Peter, the anesthesiologist in the crash room, are you the on-call neurosurgeon?"*
The surgeon: ☑ *"Yes, Jeff speaking, good morning".*
The intensive care anesthesiologist: ☑ *"I have a male patient with critical head trauma in the crash room, I'm waiting for a CT-scan".*
The surgeon: ☑ *"Okay, how is he?"*
The intensive care anesthesiologist: ☑ *"Glasgow 7, hemodynamically stable so far, he has anisocoria with pupillary dilatation in his right eye. I'm about to intubate him, and then I'll take him to the CT-scan".*
The surgeon: ☑ *"Have you let the operating room know?"*
The intensive care anesthesiologist: ☑ *"No, can you do it? Let's meet at radiology and, if there is an operating room available, we'll go straight there".*
The surgeon: ☑ *"Okay, I'll taking care of finding an operating room and warning the team; we'll meet at radiology".*
Both physicians share the same awareness of the situation and the patient's condition. In the dialogue, the two carers move up step by step towards shared knowledge.

Identify Characteristic Situations

Phraseology principles must be used at all times in the health-care field. However, various situations calling for specific provisions may be identified. A characteristic situation is a situation in which all participants have agreed beforehand on the elements that need to be verbalized.

Then on top of the general rules suggested above, extra specific rules apply.

In the aviation field, some situations are particularly codified, and specific rules apply to engine start-up, take-off, go-around procedure, etc.

In the healthcare field, some situations have already been identified, such as *the intubation of a patient admitted to a life support unit* – which happens quite often. In fact, this is a high-risk situation that generates complications in one-third of cases and may result in patient death [23].

Researchers tested a method to reduce the number of complications. A simple protocol was set up. It was made of ten points, divided between before, during and after the intubation.

Before the intubation: • presence of two operators; • filling (in the absence of pulmonary edema); • preparation of maintenance drugs for sedation; • pre-oxygenation by non-invasive ventilation (detailed procedure).

During the intubation: • rapid sequence induction (with specific drugs and dosage); • Sellick maneuver.

After the intubation: • confirmation of tracheal tube placement using capnography; • noradrenaline to start if blood pressure is diastolic <35 mmHg; • the beginning of maintenance sedation; • the beginning of protective ventilation (detailed procedure).

None of these ten recommendations was revolutionary in itself. They were in fact already implemented but in an inconsistently.

Systematic implementation of these recommendations allows us to cut the number of complications by half.

Regarding the administration of drugs, there is an existing rule called the 5 Rs:

■ the **r**ight medication
■ to the **r**ight patient
■ with the **r**ight dosage
■ at the **r**ight moment
■ on the **r**ight track

This rule is a speech guideline for issuing an oral prescription: the physician should verbalize the patient's name, the dosage, the route of administration, and when the medicine must be taken.

As for the other rules mentioned in this book, characteristic situations may also be identified on a case-by-case basis, according to different contexts and practices.

THE ARRIVAL OF PATIENTS IN POST-ANESTHESIA CARE UNITS (PACU)

A Canadian anesthesiologist explained to me a procedure applied in his anesthesia department in Montreal, relating to the arrival of patients in post-anesthesia care units (PACU). The patient, who is sometimes still asleep, "changes hands". He's no longer the operating room team's responsibility but the PACU's. The necessary transmissions usually take place upon the reception of the patient.

This is a time when the workload is high: the patient is moved from a stretcher to a hospital bed. During this transfer, the team must make sure that the drip, drainage tubes, or probes don't come off the patient's body, and set up monitoring once the patient is lying in his/her bed.

The fact that transmissions are carried out at the same time as the reception of the patient can, therefore, lead to the difficulties that have been identified.

Upon the arrival of the patient, both teams must cooperate to set him/her up. Only when both teams are free to focus on the exchange should the transmissions start.

Identify key moments

Medical teams may rely on mortality and morbidity rounds, as well as other types of feedback tools, to determine critical steps.

Each team must identify its own high-risk situations, and start using the appropriate phraseology during these key moments.

Use Structured Exchange Methods

Some characteristic situations require a series of actions. They must be performed in the right sequence, which can be difficult to memorize. In plane cockpits, there are guidebooks that provide a list of actions to be performed, step by step, in unexpected situations.

In the medical field, the use of cognitive assistance has become more and more prevalent, as it is a safe way to make sure no essential step is missed [24]. In the case of malignant hyperthermia during anesthesia, for instance, it's recommended that we use cognitive assistance – for example, a hard copy of the healthcare protocol.

This was confirmed by a research study conducted in 2012 [25]. A group of interns received training on local anesthetic poisoning (a rare and serious complication). A month later, they faced a simulated case of local anesthetic poisoning. Cognitive assistance – a checklist recounting the essential steps of the protocol – was provided to half of the interns, whereas the other half didn't get any help. The checklist group's score was much better. This study demonstrates that even though our theoretical knowledge is strong and recently acquired, it's safer to rely on a written medium, which describes the actions to be taken.

In some circumstances, reading a cognitive assistance text and performing the prescribed actions at the same time may be difficult. When facing a crisis in a plane cockpit, one of the two pilots reads the guidebook while the other takes action. This concept may be transposed to the medical field. It's then called *code reader* [26]. It's based on the principle of cognitive assistance: one of the team members reads the instructions, which reduces the workload of the caregiver executing the procedures.

Code reader = two participants
The first reads out a written review of the actions to be performed.
The second carries out the procedure.

We conducted a study on this topic. During a workshop, we taught a group of medical students how to place an intraosseous catheter on a child [27]. Two weeks later, in a simulation lab, these students faced a young child suffering from acute gastroenteritis associated with severe dehydration. In this scenario, the child had no venous access and needed an intraosseous catheter. Cognitive assistance material describing the necessary actions was available for all students. For half of them (the *code reader* group), a team member was reading the cognitive assistance material, thus acting as a *code reader*. Unsurprisingly, the *code reader* group achieved much better results than the other group. It's easier to follow a sequence of tasks if someone reads the instructions out while we carrying them out.

The *code reader* concept could be extended to other situations.

Take the Patient into Account

Whatever the type of healthcare, it's always about treating a patient. However, this fundamental precept isn't always taken into account in communication between caregivers.

The quality of the communication with a patient depends on the information he/she receives and the way he/she interprets it. That's why communication must rely on coherent speech. If the patient receives contradictory pieces of information, he/she's in doubt, fails to understand and may experience distrust. On the contrary, when caregivers agree on delivering a single logical and homogeneous message to the patient, they contribute to his/her well-being. To that end, it's important that all people caring for the patient have the same information. Good communication between caregivers is a prerequisite for good communication with the patient.

When the patient is present in the room, caregivers may communicate in different ways:

- The patient is ignored. Caregivers communicate as if the patient weren't here, intentionally or through mere negligence.
- Caregivers communicate in front of the patient, deliberately making him/her part of the exchange.
- Caregivers communicate in front of the patient without knowing it, thinking he/she's asleep or not hearing.

When two caregivers have a conversation in front of a conscious patient and don't take him/her into account, he/she may feel humiliated. Including him/her in the conversation is a way to make him/her feel that he/she's considered a human being, not only a medical case.

Ignoring a patient may also increase his/her level of stress if disturbing information – or any information that might sound alarming – is passed on. At least, caregivers must explain to the patient what they are discussing, adjust their speech, and choose user-friendly language. The patient shouldn't be placed in a position where he/she must analyze complex exchanges, as he/she might be misled and draw the wrong conclusions. He/she should never hear any diagnosis or decision regarding a treatment in the course of conversation from which he/she is excluded. The information the patient receives must be validated, interpreted and explained. Let's not forget that communication in itself is part of the field of therapeutics, through its tranquilizing and placebo effects as well as through its impact on the adherence to care and treatment [18].

Other less-easy-to-identify situations are to be dealt with cautiously. It can happen that caregivers presume the patient isn't listening; for instance, when a conversation takes place just outside the patient's room. Caregivers consider that they're far enough from the patient, whereas, in reality, he/she can hear everything or part of their conversation. The exchanged information may, once again, have a strong impact the patient, on his/her understanding of his/her condition, on his/her well-being and the quality of the way his/she is cared for. The risk always lies in the patient interpreting information that he/she might misunderstand, thus fostering a feeling of insecurity.

In other cases, caregivers may wrongly believe that the patient is asleep, but, their conversation might still be overheard and listened to.

A German team demonstrated that a patient can "hear" without remembering what he/she heard [28]. Explicit memory can be differentiated from implicit memory.

All patients participating in the study had general anesthesia for cardiac surgery. A tape recording telling a short version of Robinson Crusoe was played to the test-group (30 patients), whereas no recording was played to the control group (15 patients).

None of the 45 patients had any intraoperative memories that could be verbalized. None of them had "explicit memorization".

Researchers then conducted an implicit-memory test. The patients were asked: *"What does the word Friday bring to your mind?"* The usual answers were: *"approach of the weekend"*, *"last day of the week"*, *"fish for the dinner"*. For 7 out of the 30 patients from the test-group, *Friday* was related to Robinson

Crusoe. None of the 15 patients from the control group mentioned Robinson Crusoe.

The patient is always present

Caregivers often face patients who are seemingly asleep. Since their true level of consciousness is ignored, as well as how likely they are to remember what's being said, a question arises: what's the point of talking to a patient, knowing that he/she won't answer and that it's probably useless?

An anesthesiologist/intensive care colleague of mine told me that he discussed the matter with his team. His answer to this type of question is: *"Talk to the patients as if they were awake. It might not do them any good, but it can't hurt them. What is certain is that it will do you good"*.

More generally, everyone would like to know what's being said behind one's back. Therefore, it's important to respect the patient even though he/she's not here, and always speak as if he/she were present.

Chapter 4

Pitfalls and Touchy Situations

The implementation of the rules of phraseology doesn't prevent the onset of difficulties related to the functioning of any human group: hostility, tensions, conflicts of interests, struggle for power, self-image issues, seduction, etc.

Although inevitable, these problems must be dealt with insofar as they could be detrimental to the care, and therefore to the patient. To that end, we should always look to *"stick to the facts and keep away from emotions"* and to *"choose the right distance, not too close, not too far"* [29].

Franck Bernard and Hervé Musellec remind us that *"Conflict is only a nuisance insofar as it leads to a dead-end. Properly dealt with, it may allow [us] to go forward and reinforce the alliance"* [18].

Admit Your Ignorance

Here is the situation I faced. A intern calls me about a hypotensive patient. In order to assess the seriousness of the case,

I ask him if the patient is mottled. The intern clearly answers no. When I visit the patient, I take-off the sheets and realize that the patient is mottled. The intern who called me hadn't examined the patient's lower limbs and filled gaps in his knowledge with the most plausible piece of information he had.

The intern's mistake can be accounted for. He didn't look for the mottling, so he didn't see it, and in his mind there was none.

For cultural reasons, it's difficult to answer: *"I don't know, I didn't examine the patient enough"*. Nevertheless, this is how the intern should have answered. Passing on a piece of information that we aren't sure of may have critical consequences.

One may also alter reality without even being aware of it.

Memory is an imperfect mental process. The experience of the situation erases the details [30]. We hold on to what is felt rather than the accurate course of events. Details are forgotten, and blanks are sometimes filled with pieces of inaccurate information that are nonetheless consistent with our narrative sense of memory. Memory is a dynamic phenomenon well-known in the judiciary: eyewitnesses often prove untrustworthy, in spite of their good faith.

This may have significant implications in healthcare. When passing on information, such as a patient's medical record, we do it from memory. It is, therefore, necessary to keep in mind that memory is unreliable to avoid filling gaps in our knowledge and to remain factual as far as possible.

It's also a cultural issue. We should value caregivers who are able to determine what they know for sure and what they don't, and who only share information of which they are certain.

Avoiding admission of one's ignorance often leads us to fill in the gaps in our knowledge with incorrect information, while verbalizing it leads to awareness and leaves room for action.

> Do not replace ignorance with questionable information

In the ER

A intern works with a nurse on a morphine poisoning case. The antidote for morphine, naloxone, must be injected. Its commercial name is Narcan©. The intern and the nurse start looking for Narcan© in the ER pharmacy and find Narcozep©. Neither of them is familiar with this drug but the name is similar to the one they're searching for.

The intern: ☒ *"I think it's the right medicine. What do you think?"*
The nurse: ☒ *"Yes, I think you're right; this must be it".*
The intern: ☒ *"Okay, let's take it".*

It's confirmation bias: the intern suggested that it was the right drug, trying to dismiss the possibility that they had found the wrong drug. In spite of his own doubts, the nurse reassures the intern that his first hypothesis is correct, because he doesn't dare to admit his ignorance or contradict the physician.

They eventually inject the drug, which effects are opposed to those of the molecule they were initially looking for, and the patient's intoxication worsens.

The intern: ☑ *"I was looking for Narcan©, the name is similar. Do you know of this drug?"*
The nurse: ☑ *"No, I'm not sure about this medicine."*
The nurse: ☑ *"Okay, let's look and check in a pharmacology book to see if it's the same".*

> *"I don't know"* is a valid element of communication

Express Disagreement

When a team is involved in medical treatment, the analysis of the situation may differ according to the various points of view. A disagreement may emerge regarding the action to be taken. In a plane cockpit, the final decision is the pilot-in-command. In healthcare, it's the physician responsible for the patients. On several occasions, there have been accidents due to significant mistakes made by the person in charge, while other team members had clearly identified those mistakes. The right solution wasn't spoken, heard, or taken into consideration.

Crisis Resource Management (CRM) demonstrates that dealing with a crisis takes a confident and articulate leader. Accidents are often due to the lack of authority in a team. But a good leader must also be a good listener and remain open-minded while he/she directs. This is what it takes to strike an overall balance.

Culture change in the aviation field occurred as a consequence of the Tenerife accident.

In the KLM cockpit, just before accelerating, the flight engineer alerts the captain: *"Are we sure the runway is clear?"* The control tower never actually issued any take-off clearance, and the radio transmissions leave the situation of the Pan Am aircraft unclear. But the captain ignores the doubt with a simple *"Yes, of course"*. The flight engineer doesn't insist.

The captain had 11,700 flight hours of experience. He was a chief instructor on 747 aircraft, chief of the KLM training department and a seminal figure in the company. He had certified himself as the co-pilot on the 747, and his personality probably played a part in the absence of disagreement in the cockpit.

After this accident, the importance of expressing disagreement became vital.

In healthcare, we already mentioned Elaine Bromiley's case. The nurse who said that a tracheotomy set was available couldn't get the attention of the physician in charge. Had she managed to do so, she could have expressed her disagreement with the chosen treatment.

Upon the video analysis of this situation in the simulation lab, a consensus formed, as previously mentioned: the nurse should have drawn attention.

But let's imagine that she managed to do so. Then what could she possibly say?

A possibility naturally comes to mind: the nurse should have told the doctor, *"You must perform a tracheotomy"*. However, this scenario doesn't seem realistic in our current healthcare culture. Moreover, it's not entirely appropriate because the nurse didn't present any arguments to support her proposition, and because it creates confusion in the caregivers' roles.

There is an important difference between giving instructions and expressing a concern by proposing an idea

A more acceptable strategy would be to say, *"I think your patient needs a tracheotomy, what do you think?"* This is a better line insofar as the caregivers' roles are respected, the idea is clearly expressed and it's more likely to be heard. However, the proposition is still not discussed.

Here is what the nurse could have said:

> *"Your patient can't be intubated, nor ventilated. She's been hypoxic for several minutes; I think she needs a tracheotomy. I have the equipment with me. What do you think?"*

In order to express disagreement, we may resort to different tools: draw attention, use the right tone of voice, use the SBAR tool, ask to close the communication loop.

The Fall Off the Cliff

In May 2010, the Air India 812 flight is getting ready to land at Mangalore airport. It's a tricky maneuver because the runway is located in a high-elevation zone and ends with a cliff after a few meters of clearance. A precise approach path must be followed.

Several kilometers before reaching the airport, the co-pilot realizes that the path isn't suitable. He repeatedly tells the pilot that landing needs to be canceled, but his recommendation isn't followed. The plane should have touched down the ground at the beginning of the runway to have enough time to brake. Eventually, it touches down in the middle of the runway and falls off the cliff.

In the accident report, the relationship between the pilot and the co-pilot is examined.

Their behavior is not appropriate: both of them talk too little, the pilot is too authoritative and the co-pilot can't manage to properly express his disagreement and argue his point. The document, "Trans-Cockpit Authority Gradient" accounts for this phenomenon. This gradient shouldn't be too close to zero, because there must always be a leader. But it shouldn't be too deep either, so everyone can still express their opinions. In the Air India aircraft's case, this gradient was far too important; the pilot was too authoritarian and the co-pilot too submissive.

Sometimes, disagreement isn't even put into words. The quality of the authority gradient isn't enough to prevent difficulties.

Whether it emanates from a certainty or a simple doubt, disagreement needs to be verbalized. This nuanced expression mustn't be perceived as an impediment to carrying out the treatment. Whether it produces an effect or not, it may invigorate an operating team, by rectifying or backing up a choice.

At the Simulation Laboratory
Here is a clinical case that we often use in simulations, and that induces, at least half of the time, a typical error of communication. We submit this case to two learners who are to become a team: a very young anesthesiologist intern (in first or second year) and an experienced nurse/assistant anesthesiologist (with at least five years of experience). The scenario unfolds as follows: the on-call team starts at 5 pm and must sedate M. Empty, 50 years old, who has been complaining of pain in the appendicular region for the last 48 hours. A comedian plays the part of the surgeon. The diagnosis was made late the evening before, and the surgeon wanted to operate in the morning, but there was no available operating room. So he waited all day to proceed. The anesthesia file is available and shows no particular risk. A tray of medicines is ready. It contains propofol and succinylcholine/suxamethonium. The patient has a drip (iv access). His vital parameters are the following: Blood pressure (BP) 98/42 mmHg, heart rate (HR) 128/min.

The intern, ready for the injection: *"I'm giving propofol, succinylcholine/suxamethonium".*
The nurse/assistant anesthesiologist (close to the patient's head to intubate): ☒ *"Are you sure?"*
The intern interprets the nurse/assistant anesthesiologist's sentence as validation and proceeds to the injection. However, as the nurse/ assistant anesthesiologist had noticed, but without saying it, that the patient is hypovolemic. His blood pressure suddenly and deeply drops right after the injection. This phenomenon was predictable for an experienced professional. The nurse/assistant anesthesiologist, through the question, "Are you sure?", was expressing a doubt.

The intern, ready for the injection: *"I'm giving propofol, succinylcholine/suxamethonium".*
The nurse/assistant anesthesiologist: ☑ *"I think the patient is hypovolemic. In my opinion, it's necessary to make a filling before putting him to sleep, and to choose another induction drug, such as ketamine or etomidate".*

> Don't keep your doubts to yourself

Whether it emanates from a certainty or a simple doubt, it is necessary to verbalize a disagreement. This nuanced expression should not be seen as a barrier to the flow of care. Whether or not it is followed by an effect, it can energize a team during care, making it possible to rectify or consolidate a choice.

Apply Non-Violent Communication

Conflicts in a team may undermine the quality of a patient's treatment.

A method was developed to reduce the conflict and the suffering caused by miscommunications. It's called non-violent communication (NVC). It's not specific to medicine: this technique was developed in the 1970s by American psychologist Marshall Rosenberg [31].

According to this method, any relationship should be based on empathy, along with harmony and respect. Marshall Rosenberg proposes a four-point structured method, where the major goal is not to judge other people.

Where there is conflict or tension, being right and respected, influencing other people's behavior and testing one's power aren't the major concerns. First and foremost, the patient must remain the central focus, and be kept away from the conflict. NVC is a useful tool in such a situation: there are no accusations, just requests. It creates an atmosphere prone to communication, with nothing left unsaid.

The method is a four-step process:

- describe what I observe
- express how I feel and cope with it, speaking in the first person

- express what I need or value
- make a request

Observations
Feelings
Needs
Requests

This protocol doesn't have to be systematically implemented. It's just a tool that caregivers may use in tense situations.

When I describe what I'm observing, I need to remain factual and say something that leaves no room for interpretation. Example: the patient is coughing and has a fever.

When I express how I feel, I share a personal feeling. It may be difficult to say and to cope with it. However, it creates a connection with the other person. For instance, we should say *"I feel angry"*, instead of *"You're getting angry"*.

When I express a need, I also take a personal initiative: it's something I don't project onto another person.

Last, when I make a request, it must be as clear as possible to improve efficiency.

CONFLICT BETWEEN
ANESTHESIOLOGIST AND SURGEON

An ENT surgeon works in a hospital with several anesthesiologists.

For this surgeon, some anesthesiologists are not qualified for the surgery he performs. He would like to work only with anesthesiologists who are well versed in ENT surgery. Anesthesiologists, who work alternately with several surgical specialties, do not wish to specialize and want to keep a homogeneous and versatile team. They dig their heels in and oppose the ENT's request. This situation creates tension that might have been avoided.

The surgeon's request, which was made without following the steps of "observation, feelings, needs, request" beforehand, may be perceived as interfering or accusing:

"I don't want to work with Dr X, Dr Y, or Dr Z".

On the contrary, NVC allows us to understand the surgeon's needs and meet them with a satisfying answer.
The surgeon could express:

■ an observation:

"On the last rigid laryngoscopy, I couldn't perform the exam nor the biopsies because the patient started an apnea, desaturated, and had to be intubated. On a different occasion, I couldn't perform my work because the patient was moving too much. However, this technique works with some anesthesiologists. But not with all of them".

■ his feelings:

"I feel uneasy towards the patient because I couldn't provide medical care".

■ his needs:

"I need patients who don't move".

■ his request:

"Would it be possible to work exclusively with anesthesiologists with whom I systematically manage to operate without problems?"

The person in charge of the anesthesiologists might then conclude:

> *"I understand your request. I'm going to write an anesthesia protocol that corresponds to the technique of the most efficient anesthesiologists, and ask everyone to respect it".*

Chapter 5

The Implementation

Each of us may use phraseology in his/her own way; clarify messages, choose a meaningful attitude, adjust one's tone of voice to a situation, ask to close the communication loop and develop personal tools to express an opinion or disagreement.

However, phraseology is meant to be used to the greatest possible extent, to as wide an audience as possible. The goal of this book is not only to raise awareness, but also to induce a change in practice.

Long is the road from knowledge to implementation. Cultural or organizational obstacles may interfere. There is a significant gap between putting the concept into words and implementing it.

The implementation of the phraseology may, therefore, require a real effort and the application of certain methods.

Don't Be Firm or Excessive

As a clinician, I don't entice people to turn phraseology into a dogma, nor to implement it authoritatively. Misusing this tool might lead caregivers to dismiss it.

The key question is not *"Am I speaking well?"* but *"Is the patient well cared for?"* This science of communication is a tool that still needs to prove its value through experimentation.

Any attempt at normalization could have adverse effects.

In order to be efficient, phraseology must progressively become a habit, but not a constraint.

It shouldn't conflict with a positive atmosphere within a team, nor be detrimental to working conditions by imposing rules when they aren't necessary. For instance, it's no use limiting the background noise when it's not disturbing.

People should be made aware of the relation between the effort made to implement a new rule and its benefit. When perceiving a tangible benefit, caregivers tend to be more compliant. Therefore, critical points are to be tackled first. We can't use a ready-made and controlled system of communication at all times. In fact, each situation may require its own rules.

The purpose of phraseology is not to judge others. Indeed, for the sake of a culture of safety, communication around any mistake should be valued and used to improve ourselves.

Given the number of available rules, we may become afraid of not talking well enough, and therefore find ourselves speaking less – which would be entirely counterproductive. A team of Swiss researchers studied the performances of medical teams in simulations. They noticed that the best performing teams were those in which caregivers communicated the most, regardless of the content of what was said [32]. Hence a new rule: *"First, do not keep silent"* [33]. It's not about sterilizing the language, but about freeing our voices and making them more efficient.

> Phraseology must be a help, not a constraint

Let's Change Things Together

Currently, communication between caregivers has no established rules. That's why the implementation of medical phraseology represents a change that can be considered over a wide range of scales. A medical care professional may autonomously choose the way he/she communicates. If a group makes this change in communication – whether it's a medical team, a healthcare facility, or a larger community – then this evolution occurs on a collective scale.

In healthcare, as in other lines of work, collective change isn't easy nor rational: in spite of the advantages it provides, it might not be accepted nor implemented at once.

For instance, hand washing represents a change that slowly became essential in medical care. Its fundamental purpose was discovered in 1846 by Hungarian obstetrician Ignace Semmelweis. However, the principle of handwashing was dismissed or ignored for many years. Today, the usefulness of handwashing is widely acknowledged, although its implementation still requires some effort in terms of organization. As Gawande reminds us [34], this rule of handwashing is well-respected in the operating room but much less by the patient's bed.

The use of a checklist in the operating unit represents a more recent example of a difficult change. Its efficiency is proven, acknowledged and unquestioned. Yet, its implementation remains partial and uncertain [35].

Researchers, in fields other than healthcare, have theorized the steps of change on a collective scale.

In his book *Leading Change*, author and economist John Kotter explains that the outcome of major change initiatives – whether regarding quality improvement or cultural change – is often very limited [36]. According to him, change ought to be considered a process, not an event.

Each new step toward change is based on the previous ones, and a major change may take years to come through. Pressure from management to accelerate the process leads to short-circuits and causes failure. Organizations are more likely to implement change successfully when they understand its different steps and key-points.

John Kotter describes an eight-step process.

- 1. *Create a sense of urgency.* Identify untapped opportunities and convince your team that the status quo is more dangerous than change. Don't underestimate the difficulty of getting out of one's comfort zone; risk can be crippling.
- 2. *Build a guiding coalition.* Identify people that are truly convinced about the importance of change, and form a team you can rely on.

- 3. *Form a strategic vision and initiatives.* Have a clear vision of the future you're heading to.

- 4. *Enlist a volunteer army.* Focus on transmitting your vision. Try to spread your vision by all possible means and teach new behaviors through the example of your guiding team.
- 5. *Enable action by removing barriers.* Make all participants feel autonomous and responsible for these new behaviors. It's about putting your vision into practice and fostering new ideas. If important individuals in key-positions are reluctant to change, they might jeopardize the process.
- 6. *Generate short-term wins.* Plan and value every single little win, and encourage people contributing to these small changes. In medical care, simple targets may be defined: introduce yourself and mention your location systematically when picking up the phone for a month.

Then it will be difficult to go back to the way you
behaved before.
■ 7. *Sustain acceleration.* Create more ambitious changes.
Once credibility is earned through small changes, rely on
it to help the system evolve globally. However, don't take
the change for granted yet.
■ 8. *Institute change.* It's about embedding new practices in
the corporate culture. In the medical field, for instance,
we might consider that the early institutionalization of the
checklist in the operating room was a mistake. A more
progressive implementation might have allowed care professionals to accept it more readily. [37]

Kotter's eight-step process is questionable in several respects.
It's based on the acceptance of change, which is arguable;
it's very linear because the sequence of steps must be strictly
observed; and it's an authoritative *top-down* management
model, which isn't the only possible configuration.

Change isn't a self-evident process: it may fail, and there are
methods to support it.

In order to implement phraseology, it's appropriate to follow a well-established change management method.

One can resort to a model slightly simpler than Kotter's:
Lewin's 3-Stage Model of Change:

■ Unfreezing (since many people naturally resist change,
the goal is to create awareness of how the current situation is hindering the organization)
■ Changing (implementation of the change, adjustment to
new behaviors, processes and ways of thinking)
■ Refreezing (reinforcing, stabilizing and solidifying the new
situation after the change)

This model is based on the ice block metaphor. If you're
intending to reshape it, you must unfreeze it first. Regarding

phraseology, let's recognize that we don't communicate efficiently enough.

Then, if you want the new shape to last, you must solidify the change. In the communication field, it's about finding a way to maintain the use of new practices in the future.

In the 1940s, Kurt Lewin described change resistance and how a group of individuals tended to switch back to its former habits.

Acquisition of new rules

The stages of change are also the stages of learning.

Once a change is learned, whether on an individual or collective scale, it becomes effortless.

Many examples in our daily life show how easy it may be to use a new rule once it's "embedded". When driving a stick-shift car on a daily basis, we step on the clutch without thinking about it. It's become automatic. The cognitive load involved in this action is very low. However, during the learning stage, this move required concentration and a back-and-forth process between mistakes and corrections. If you ask an automatic car driver to drive a stick-shift vehicle, he/she'll face this learning phenomenon.

Medical phraseology between caregivers is likely to undergo the same process. The learning stage will entail an increase in cognitive load and a mistake/correction back-and-forth process. However, we can reasonably expect that this new behavior will soon become an effortless automatism. In the long run, the absence of phraseology might even be disturbing. If you're driving your car while your seatbelt isn't fastened, you'll feel that something is missing. If you're used to driving a stick-shift car and switch to an automatic vehicle, you'll automatically step on an imaginary clutch. If you're a surgeon, you can't operate if you haven't washed your hands.

Create Your Own Rules

The easiest-to-apply rules are those we create ourselves. This is the *bottom-up* model: rules are not issued by any authority from outside the working area but emanate from in-field feedback.

Brigid Gillespie demonstrated that the more involved the doctors were in the implementation of the checklist, the better they adjusted it to the context and their specialty and the better it worked [35].

On its website, the WHO proposes a checklist for operating rooms and mentions that any modification should be encouraged. Making this tool their own entices medical professionals to feel more responsible.

This method can be used to implement phraseology.

Caregivers already have a number of ways to change their practice autonomously: morbidity and mortality conferences, drafting an update to service charters, bibliographic meetings ...

The French National Authority for Health (Haute Autorité de santé) defines morbidity and mortality conferences as

> *a systemic and retrospective collective analysis of cases marked by the occurrence of death, complications or any event that might have been detrimental to the patient's health, and whose goal is to implement and follow-up on actions in order to improve the patients' treatments and care safety.*

This analysis is conducted by the teams in charge, and no external individual may interfere. The reports are made anonymous and not added to the patient's medical file.

In this global analysis, phraseology may represent a new approach, a new focus for discussion with a view to understand mistakes and correct them. In that case, we shall use a new rule, not because we were asked to do so, but because it's in the patients' best interest.

In the aviation field, any important field feedback must not only be shared with the members of the airline company involved but also with other companies using the same planes. To that end, large-scale broadcasting systems have been created, such as the newsletter *Callback*. In the medical field, feedback broadcasting systems (*see* http://www.patientsafetydatabase.com/) are currently being set up and will probably represent a valuable source of information to confirm or improve the rules of phraseology.

The main issue regarding incident analysis and field feedback is that they are based on medical care professionals' memory and the patient's medical file. Yet, memory is fallible: in the simulation lab, we noticed that learners don't remember exactly the words they pronounced. In aviation, the use of "black boxes" solved this matter. Indeed, these flight recorders contain precise elements regarding what was said. Under the leadership of Dr Grantcharov, a team of Canadian researchers implemented a "surgical black box". This device allows for recording and analyzing a large number of parameters in the operating room [39], including conversations. This feedback tool is meant to improve performance. In the future, data analysis conducted through the prism of phraseology might help us make progress.

Morbidity and mortality conferences or accident analysis are retrospective analyses: we wait for the accident to occur before we can prevent it from happening again. It would make more sense to think, before an accident occurs, of better methods of communication to identify high-risk situations.

Conclusion

Communication is a complex process affected by both internal (cultural and personal values) and external factors (role, a position of authority) [40]. More than an individual skill, phraseology encompasses a range of rules which, put into context, represents a collective skill. Within this frame, these rules could be incorporated into Medical Team Training programs and to some national health authorities' projects, such as the Teamwork Continuous Improvement program conducted by the French High Health Authority.

Whether we use it for CRM or the checklist, phraseology meets safety concerns in a context of healthcare complexification. In order to keep up with the constant increase in knowledge about pathologies and the ever-growing number of possible procedures and available medicines, caregivers need to call on external resources. Cognitive science teaches us that knowledge is not to be found within a single individual but in social and environmental interaction. This is the situated cognition theory [41]. Therefore, the community becomes a necessary resource. Phraseology represents an efficient way to mobilize this resource. From a broader perspective, we could use other resources (that we won't develop here), such as:

■ his/her environment (ergonomics)
■ cognitive aids, which are used much less in the healthcare field compared to the aviation field

Being competent implies the ability to admit that our skills are limited. In healthcare, incompetence could lead someone to take responsibility for an act he/she couldn't control.

Admitting partial incompetence will entice medical care professionals to mobilize external resources. To that end, certain values need to be embraced, such as those described by Atul Gawande [42] for checklist acceptance and implementation. First comes humility: complying with procedures is accepting that we may make mistakes. Then comes discipline: all rules must apply, every day, to all patients. Watch out for accidents when you don't comply with the rules. In the end, it comes down to teamwork: everyone has to play his/her part, no one can act alone.

Afterword

Throughout history, there has always been a concern for sharing a common language among caregivers. Over the generations, a true medical language has developed, sometimes mixing Latin and Greek. This language learned during medical and paramedical studies is most often used to refer to a patient's condition, disease, or care strategy. It rarely concerns actions or procedures.

Modern medicine, which is increasingly complex, creates a hyper-specialization of knowledge. While teamwork has become a key issue in health safety, hyper-specialists have created their own medical jargon, sometimes not understood by their colleagues or nurses. In addition, today's hospital staff come from very diverse socio-cultural categories, with a multitude of professionals working for the same patient, each with their own communication codes. Misunderstandings and inaccuracies are a major source of medical error. The difficulty of synchronizing healthcare teams around sometimes complex procedures has now become a critical issue in all areas of healthcare. Effective communication between the public is certainly one of the most important tools for improving health safety.

The book written by Dr. Jérôme Cros of the University Hospital of Limoges is an open door. It allows a first step toward the establishment of a health phraseology, a standardization of communication that would be taught and shared by all health professionals. The importance of this work is obvious, as the examples given by Dr. Cros demonstrate. It proposes a methodology for making our communication more effective. This book will most likely be a reference in the years to come, and will hopefully generate a lot of work.

However, we still have important steps to take. A description of the risky procedures requiring standardized communication must be made. While it seems obvious that in "critical" environments – such as the operating room, intensive care or emergencies, procedures (such as orotracheal intubation or clamping a large vessel) must be subject to mandatory team synchronization and optimized communication, there are probably many other areas of application to be specified. Like aeronautics, this work will have to be done by the teams themselves, using feedback from in the field. Once this inventory has been compiled, it will then be necessary to verify its application in daily practice, and then allow it to evolve and adapt to the increasingly rapid changes in medicine and society. The use of standardized communication could thus become one of the "quality" criteria, monitored on a daily basis for the benefit of patient safety. It is up to each of us to train ourselves in the use of this medical phraseology and to convey Doctor Cros' book to our medical teams.

Professor Thomas Geeraerts
Professor of Hospital Practitioners Universities in Anesthesia and Resuscitation Director of the Toulouse Institute of Health Simulation Toulouse University Hospital, Toulouse 3-Paul Sabatier University, Toulouse, France

References

1. Cooper GE, White MD, Lauber JK. Resource management on the flight deck. San Francisco; 1980, pp. 1–255. Available from: https://ntrs.nasa.gov/archive/nasa/casi.ntrs.nasa.gov/198000 13796.pdf.
2. Gaba DM, Fish KJ, Howard SK. *Crisis Management in Anesthesiology.* Churchill Livingstone; 1994.
3. Gaba DM. Crisis resource management and teamwork training in anaesthesia. *British Journal of Anaesthesia.* 2010;105(1):3–6.
4. Kohn LT, Corrigan JM, Donaldson MS. *To Err is Human: Building a Safer Health System.* Washington, DC: The National Academies Press; 2000.
5. Haynes AB, Weiser TG, Berry WR, Lipsitz SR, Breizat A-HS, Dellinger EP, et al. A surgical safety checklist to reduce morbidity and mortality in a global population. *New England Journal of Medicine.* 2009;360(5):491–9.
6. Sutcliffe KM, Lewton E, Rosenthal MM. Communication failures: An insidious contributor to medical mishaps. *Academic Medicine* . 2004;79(2):186–94.
7. Haller G, Laroche T, Clergue F. Evènements indésirables et problèmes de communication en périopératoire. *Annales française d'anesthesie et de réanimation.* Elsevier Masson SAS. 2011;30(12):923–9.
8. International Civil Aviation Organization. *Manual of Radiotelephony.* 4th ed.; 2007.
9. Beckett CD, Kipnis G. Collaborative communication: Integrating SBAR to improve quality/patient safety outcomes. 2009;31(5):19–28.

10. Balliu C. *Le langage de la médecine: Les mots pour le dire.* Bruxelles; 2005, pp. 1–6.
11. IFR phraseology Version 1.3; 26 July 2015 © IVAO HQ Training Department.
12. Rudigoz R-C, Huissoud C, Delecour L, Thevenet S, Dupont C. [Non elective cesarean section: Use of a color code to optimize management of obstetric emergencies]. *Bulletin de l'Académie Nationale de Médecine.* 2014;198(6):1123–38.
13. Cushing S. *Fatal Words: Communication Clashes and Aircraft Crashes.* University of Chicago Press; 1997.
14. Haig KM, Sutton S, Whittington J. SBAR: A shared mental model for improving communication between clinicians. *Joint Commission Journal on Quality and Patient Safety.* 2006;32(3):167–75.
15. De Meester K, Verspuy M, Monsieurs KG, Van Bogaert P. SBAR improves nurse–physician communication and reduces unexpected death: A pre and post intervention study. *Resuscitation.* European Resuscitation Council, American Heart Association, Inc., and International Liaison Committee on Resuscitation. ~ Published by Elsevier Ireland Ltd. 2013;84(9):1192–6.
16. Richard C, Lussier M-T. *La communication professionnelle en santé.* ERPI - Le Renouveau Pédagogique Editions; 2016.
17. Bouquerel R, Ponsonnard S, Sengès P, Nathan N, Cros J. Recours à une assistance circulatoire de type extracorporeal life support dans le cas d'un arrêt cardio-respiratoire réfractaire compliquant une embolie amniotique. *Anesthésie & Réanimation. Société française d'anesthésie et de réanimation (Sfar).* 2016;2(3):177–80.
18. Bernard F, Musellec H. La communication dans le soin : Hypnose médicale et techniques relationnelles. *Arnette.* 2013.
19. McEwen A, Kraszewski S. *Communication Skills for Adult Nurses.* McGraw-Hill Education; 2010.
20. Bromiley M. Have you ever made a mistake? *Bulletin of the Royal College of Anaesthetists.* 2008;48:2242–5.
21. Tajima A. *Fatal Miscommunication: English in Aviation Safety. World Englishes.* 24th ed. Blackwell Publishing Ltd/Inc; 2004;23(3):451–70.

22. Enser M, Moriceau J, Abily J, Damm C, Occhiali E, Besnier E, et al. Background noise lowers the performance of anaesthesiology residents' clinical reasoning when measured by script concordance. *European Journal of Anaesthesiology.* 2017;34(7):464–70.

23. Jaber S, Jung B, Corne P, Sebbane M, Muller L, Chanques G, et al. An intervention to decrease complications related to endotracheal intubation in the intensive care unit: A prospective, multiple-center study. *Intensive Care Medicine.* 2009;36(2):248–55.

24. Gaba DM. Perioperative cognitive aids in anesthesia. *Anesthesia and Analgesia.* 2013;117(5):1033–6.

25. Neal JM, Hsiung RL, Mulroy MF, Halpern BB, Dragnich AD, Slee AE. ASRA checklist improves trainee performance during a simulated episode of local anesthetic systemic toxicity. *Reg Anesth Pain Med.* 2012;37(1):8–15.

26. Power DJ, Boet S, Bould MD. Code reader. Simulation in healthcare. *The Journal of the Society for Simulation in Healthcare.* 2012;7(2):136–7.

27. Gilbert G, Haziza G, Pihan G, Tahir A, Ponsonnard S, Cros J. *Évaluation en simulation haute-fidélité de l'impact du Code Reader sur la pose d'une voie intra- osseuse chez l'enfant.* Paris; 2016, pp. 1–2.

28. Schwender D, Kaiser A, Klasing S, Peter K, Pöppel E. Midlatency auditory evoked potentials and explicit and implicit memory in patients undergoing cardiac surgery. *Anesthesiology.* 1994;80(3):493–501.

29. Travers V, Cuche H, Gaertner E. *Anesthésiste-Réanimateur/ Chirurgien: Un seul bloc.* Arnette; 2013.

30. Stiegler MP, Tung A. Cognitive processes in anesthesiology decision making. *Anesthesiology.* 2014;120(1):204–17.

31. Rosenberg MB, Gandhi A, Rojzman C, Baut-Carlier F. *Les mots sont des fenêtres (ou des murs): Introduction à la Communication Non Violente.* Editions La Découverte; 2016.

32. Kolbe M, Burtscher MJ, Wacker J, Grande B, Nohynkova R, Manser T, et al. Speaking up is related to better team performance in simulated anesthesia inductions: An observational study. *Anesthesia and Analgesia.* 2012;115(5):1099–108.

33. Dwyer J. Primum non tacere. An ethics of speaking up. *Hastings Center Report.* 1994;24(1):13–8.
34. Gawande AA. *Better: A Surgeon's Notes on Performance.* Henry Holt and Company; 2008.
35. Gillespie BM, Marshall A. Implementation of safety checklists in surgery: A realist synthesis of evidence. *Implementation Science.* 2015;10(1):1–14.
36. Kotter JP. Leading change: Why transformation efforts fail. *Harvard Business Review.* 2007.
37. Levy SM, Senter CE, Hawkins RB, Zhao JY, Doody K, Kao LS, et al. Implementing a surgical checklist: More than checking a box. *Surgery.* 2012;152(3):331–6.
38. Lewin K. Frontiers in group dynamics. *Human Relations.* 1947;1(1):5–41.
39. Moulton D. Surgical black box may sew up malpractice cases. *CMAJ.* 2015;187(11):794–4.
40. d'Agincourt-Canning LG, Kissoon N, Singal M, Pitfield AF. Culture, communication and safety: Lessons from the airline industry. *Indian Journal of Pediatrics.* 2010;78(6):703–8.
41. Artino AR Jr. It's not all in your head: Viewing graduate medical education through the lens of situated cognition. *Journal of Graduate Medical Education.* 2013;5(2):177–9.
42. Gawande AA. *The Checklist Manifesto.* New York: Picador; 2009, 215 p.

Index

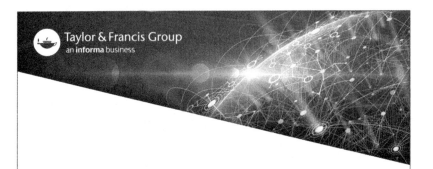